NO-ONE LAND:
Israel / Palestine 2000-2002

NO-ONE LAND:
Israel / Palestine 2000-2002

Henry Ralph Carse

ZIGGURAT BOOKS
International

No-One Land: Israel / Palestine 2000-2002
Copyright ©2010 by Henry Ralph Carse

All photographs by Henry Ralph Carse

All rights reserved. Except for brief passages quoted in a newspaper, magazine, radio, or television program, no part of this book may be reproduced in any form or by any means, electronic or mechanical, including photocopying and recording, or by any information storage and retrieval system, without permission in writing from the Publisher.

Front cover photograph: Separation Wall near Bethlehem, 2010
Back cover photograph: Destroyed home in Beit Jala, 2010
Other photographs: Beit Jala, Hebron and Jerusalem, 2000-2010

UK office: 27 St. Quentin House, Fitzhugh Grove,
London SW18 3SE, England
Enquiries: zigguratbooks@orange.fr

Distributed by Central Books Ltd.
99 Wallis Road, London E9 5LN, England
Tel UK: 0845 458 9911
Fax UK: 0845 459 9912
Tel International: +44 20 8525 8800
Fax International: +44 20 8525 8879
Email: orders@centralbooks.com

Illustrated Edition

ISBN 978-0-9561038-8-8

Henry Ralph Carse, practical theologian, pilgrim and scholar, has lived in the Middle East for forty years. A graduate of Hebrew University (Jerusalem), The General Theological Seminary (New York), and the University of Kent at Canterbury, his Ph.D. thesis in theology is a postmodern study of pilgrim narratives. He is the Founder of "Kids4Peace" in Jerusalem and "Kids4Peace USA," bringing together Israeli and Palestinian youngsters of three faiths for encounter and dialogue across the lines of conflict.

For my children

CONTENTS

Preface: A Walk in No-One Land 1

Dreams or Nightmares 5

Letter to an Israeli Soldier 10

November in Jerusalem 13

Some Bad Wizards 23

Cages 28

No-One Land 38

Get the Connection 46

From a Distance 56

Letter to a Palestinian Christian 62

A Home in Anata 68

Some People Marching 74

Perfectly Safe Rubble 82

Both Sides Now 88

What About the Kids 92

As If 96

Olive Trees 103

Some Holy Bullies 108

Halfway Words 114

Letter to a Muslim Colleague 119

Banalities and Blessings 123

References 133

PREFACE

A WALK IN NO-ONE LAND

These essays were written at the outbreak of the Second *Intifada* – the Palestinian uprising of a decade ago. The conflict continues, even as compassion-fatigue renders it invisible. A Palestinian family lives in a wire mesh cage in Hebron, Arabs in Jerusalem become fugitives on their way to work, a soldier refuses to serve in the Occupied Territories, a bus driver plays Samson in a fatal drama, an Israeli bride and groom are plunged into chaos when their wedding hall collapses, wizards of war play their power games, a daughter is drafted into the Army of Israel as her father joins the nonviolent resistance, a pilgrim takes a morning stroll along the "Green Line" between bombs and croissants, people of faith search in vain for a conscience, youngsters become soldiers, snipers, suicide bombers, executioners and martyrs, enemies and, sometimes, friends.

If these essays can show anything, it is that nothing adds up. There is a deep flaw here, a wound in human nature through which the fear and killing flow unstaunched. This should not happen, not for the sake of security or liberty or revenge or guilt or sovereignty. The whole thing is wrong.

I knew this unconsciously when I first arrived in the Holy Land in the afterglow of the Six Day War, as my *kibbutznik* pals showed me the ruins of Arab homes in their new citrus groves. I knew this, subliminally, in Black September when I heard the guns across the Jordan doing their gruesome work, and I knew it on Yom Kippur when we saw mountains yawning open to spew forth tanks. I knew it with growing clarity during the First *Intifada* – that unexpected "Rising Up And Shaking Off" of a whole comatose generation. I knew it during the condoned reprisals in the streets of El Arroub and Jerusalem. For a brief and weirdly photogenic moment of sticks-and-stones brutality, in a "rising up" of conscience, the world knew it too.

Just as quickly, the world forgot.

I had known the truth for long enough when the scuds arched terrifyingly over the rooftops of Jerusalem, when governments sanctioned settlements to rape the land, when checkpoints went up in the Territories, when suicide bombings intensified, and when terror hastened the construction of The Separation Wall.

These essays remain what they were: powerless but necessary realizations of a banal and baffling injustice. The script is much the same – the actors, however, change. Boys with guns become executives with computers, war wizards are writing memoirs, the daughter is married, the pilgrim has gone home. Two enigmas whose presence brooded between the lines of the original essays – Arafat and Sharon – are now not available for comment. Our fears, it seems, outlive our fear-mongers, our terror survives our terror-masters. Neither the arrogance of an Israeli leader nor the egomania of a Palestinian leader could alone plunge millions into this Kafkaesque cycle of viciousness; it was our own helplessness that sprang the trap. And now, with one of those leaders buried in Palestine and the other comatose in Israel, the viciousness still infects us like an alien impulse.

A decade has passed since the opening throes of the Second *Intifada* brought "the situation" to fever pitch. But it has been a decade of awakening for no one. We have been sobered by what we learned, but this is "newsworthy" to no one. The essays I wrote then may appropriately be re-published now, and may perhaps be heeded by no one. I wish this were not true, but no one is wiser, no one is free. Briefly, the world's glance touched the human tragedy of Israel and Palestine, and then moved on, unremarkedly, as if no one's children were in the crossfire.

Eothen, Vermont, 17 December 2009 – East Jerusalem, 21 January 2010

ESSAYS & LETTERS

DREAMS OR NIGHTMARES
Jerusalem, 15th October 2000

One thousand years ago, an Arab Jerusalemite named Muqaddasi wrote: "Jerusalem is a golden bowl filled with scorpions." More recently, a Jewish Jerusalemite, Yehuda Amichai, wrote: "The air over Jerusalem is saturated with prayers and dreams... It's hard to breathe."

Poets can see what many of us cannot: the poison and fear which we sanctify in our streets, the suffocation and terror we feed on in our heads and hearts.

Dreams can be good. They can bring us messages, tell us what is really going on. But if we are imprisoned in our dreams, they can become nightmares. We struggle to awake. Sleepwalking, traumatized, we can murder our own children, our neighbors, our city, unaware that our dreams have turned us into monsters. The harsh light of morning in Jerusalem may shatter our dark sleep, and we may sit up, look numbly at the blood on our hands, look around at the silent empty house, and weep.

On September 28th, a heavy dreamer sleepwalked with his eyes wide open, protected by a legion of sleepwalking soldiers, onto a stage called the Holy Mount. As if we had been practicing for decades, we all sprang from the wings to enact our dream reactions: rage, terror, helplessness, resistance, shock, righteous indignation, brutality. The script was perfect; the lines we shouted seemed to make so much sense. In fact, they were gibberish. We jerked and mumbled in our sleep, and our nightmares drew blood.

Was young Muhammad really riddled with live fire as he clung to his father at the Netzarim Junction? Were Yosef and Vadim really beaten to death, their mutilated bodies thrown out of the window by angry Palestinians in Ramallah? Did gangs of Jewish settlers really brutally attack their Arab neighbors in Nazareth? Did young men strap explosives to their bodies and destroy buses packed with citizens? Unspeakable scripts have been played out in these two weeks, since we all followed the sleepwalking Pied Piper into the Sea of Banality. These are the nightmares we have been weaving; it is we ourselves who have made them real. People have really been killed. They can't sleep, or dream, or wake up, ever again.

Now is the "morning after." We who are still alive are struggling to wake up. The biggest hangover of our lives awaits us at the end of this tunnel of night. We are saturated with prayers, drunk with nightmares, but, finally, our eyes are opening.

What we say and do now will determine whether we are awake or still trapped in our unconsciousness. If we gesture wildly at everyone else, blaming everyone but ourselves, keeping our faces set, unyielding to tears, unyielding to light, we can still cling to our precious and protective sleep.

We can cling to our dreams of victory. If we are Jews, we can dream of a Jewish State from the Nile to the Euphrates, a safe homeland, a land granted to us by God. We can feel good in this dream. Spasmodically, we can vilify and maim anyone who threatens to shake us awake, anyone who tries to say: "Someone is here with you! You are not the masters you think you are! Your mighty dream will not keep you safe!"

If we are Arabs, we can cling to our dream of a united homeland stretching from the Gulf to Gibraltar, free of colonies and foreigners, a safe haven from those "out there," a culture of the East where hospitality rules and where good Muslim caliphs reign. We can feel good in this dream. We can, in our sleep, brush aside or push away any unpleasant visitors who settle among us, who try to say: "We are here to stay! Your slumber is broken! You are not alone!"

If we are politically minded, we can mumble and reason and bluster: "The law is on our side. You are wrong, we are right.

You are attacking us, victimizing us, brutalizing us. We have every right to hate you..." And so forth.

If we consider ourselves spiritual, we can hum and sing and preach, quoting sacred texts that make us feel good about ourselves and bad about everyone else, texts that take on lives of their own, texts that become scorpions in our houses and heavy poisoned air in our streets, texts that kill us so softly that we don't even know we have died in our sleep and that the sacred words we obey are just the echoes of our dying fears.

As Jerusalem burns around us, we can revel in our dreams of victories – the pyrrhic victories of pyromaniacs.

Or...we can wake up to the prospect of...what?

Peace without victory.

We can stand up, throw open the windows, and see what we have done. Is there a stone that has not been thrown? Is there a type of bullet that we have not tried to shoot? Is there an obscenity that we have not forced our children to witness? Is there any heart that has not turned to stone? Can we find the energy to cry? Are our hands permanently clamped to our faces to shut out our horror? Do we have any desire left to eat, talk, work or play, to write poems or make love like real people?

If we wake up, we can still have dreams. Our dreams can be beautiful and strong; they may even become a vision. We can listen to our hearts without ripping out each other's eyes. All we have to give up is our nightmarish life, the life of sleepwalkers, the life of lonely psychotics bent on death, inhabiting cities of scorpions and unbreathable air. What is required to live in the light of day is not so impossible; not even terribly difficult. But we have to be awake to do it. If we swear allegiance to our sleep, we may never see the light of day again.

We know very well what needs to be done. Most of the West Bank and the Gaza Strip need to become a Palestinian State, and soon. Most Israeli settlements in the West Bank and Gaza need to be dismantled and evacuated. The "biblical" energy that built them can find another outlet. Maybe Abraham's children can live there (under other names) if the houses built by Israeli settlers can shelter returning Palestinian refugees. So sorry, ideological settlers, but the price of clinging to your fantasy is just too high. Take the money and move, and stop whimpering. You'll be fine.

Jerusalem needs to be shared, and the formula for that is so simple that every school child already knows it. So sorry, all you Bible thumpers and Qur'an thumpers. The price of exclusive control in this city is just too high. In our nightmares we have been paying that price too long. So move over and make room for Muslim, Jewish and Christian city councilors on the bench. Make room for two flags on the roof. Make room for a shared constitution, the hallmark of a sane society.

Move over, everyone. You'll be just fine.

Make room for democratic processes that will lead eventually to a Middle East Federation – Israel, Palestine, Jordan and Syria in economic and cultural interface. It will not come tomorrow, but it will come. Open bank accounts for the glad profits from tourism to a country that is not a Jewish Fortress or a Muslim Castle or a Christian Cemetery but a delightful modern paradise of culture and learning. Build tasteful hotels for the pilgrims who will flock to shrines that are no longer gloomy reminders of how religions hate each other.

Move over and make room. You can do it.

These last two weeks can be our last nights of nightmares – if we rouse ourselves today. Look out the window to see the first rains of blessing fall and wash the blood stains into the soft and forgiving earth. Cry for what we have all done to each other, but be ready to laugh too.

It's not the end of the world – it can be the beginning of day. But only if we first wake up.

LETTER TO AN ISRAELI SOLDIER
Jerusalem, 28th October 2000

Dear N.,

When I first heard of you, my 17-year-old daughter told me that you know a friend of hers. That was a reason to feel connected to you. That, and, of course, the nightmarish brutality we see all around us, the anger I feel in my Palestinian neighbors in East Jerusalem, the fear in my Israeli colleagues, the uneasiness I feel about not having done everything that was in my power to avert this bloodbath – all of these helped me to really pay attention to the news of your decision.

They report that you, an Israeli soldier, refused to be posted to an Israeli Defense Forces position in the Palestinian Territories occupied by Israel. Your sentence was imprisonment.

I am writing to thank you. If this is just one of hundreds of grateful letters from parents of Israeli kids who are about to be drafted, that's fine. But if this is a rare letter, then please read it carefully and treasure it. Genuine gratitude from a total stranger is a rare thing in this world.

When I arrived in Israel from the States at the age of eighteen, with my guitar and long hair and idealism, I was running away from many shadows, the least subtle of which was called Vietnam. I had graduated from high school and there was a good chance that I would be drafted. I knew that for me to go to the Far East to shoot and be shot at was completely wrong. As I was not mature enough to decide to become a conscientious objector, I bought a ticket and got out of the USA.

Israel was the place I chose. I found it more interesting than Canada, so here is where I ended up. I don't regret it, but I sure do wish I had had the guts and the brains to make a more clear-cut statement of my opposition to what was already widely recognized as an immoral military involvement.

Years later, ironically enough, when I had become an Israeli citizen, I was drafted into the IDF. I was in my thirties by that time, pretty ancient to be a soldier in Israel's army, but there I was. I did my basic training, followed by active service during the First *Intifada* in the Occupied West Bank. You know what this is all about, so you will appreciate what it means when I say that I never acted shamefully, never raised a hand against any person of any age, never fired my gun, never entered a home uninvited, and did my best every day to be a peaceful influence in my unit. Nevertheless, you can also understand when I say that I now regret having worn the uniform of Israel's Army in the Occupied Territories. If I were called to do so today, I would absolutely refuse.

It seems I won't be tested on that. I have dropped out of the IDF computers – perhaps I am no longer of interest. It is up to me to translate my regrets into a positive mode of peacemaking.

And now my daughter is seventeen. Next year she will be drafted and put on her uniform. My 15-year-old son will soon do the same, and – eventually – my youngest son as well. I can offer them advice, and even a kind of theoretical guide to right behavior for a soldier with a conscience. But what I cannot offer them is a contemporary role model for right action at this very moment. They will always feel that my experiences, however worthwhile, were good for "way back then," and may not apply to their decisions *now*. I may know in my heart what they should do, but I cannot take the risk for them. I can assure them, as they stand for truth and moral behavior, that they are not alone in their generation in seeking a way out of this demoralizing occupation of another people and into a more honest future. Still, I cannot actually show them the way, as much as I would like to, simply because I am their *Abba*, not their peer. I am too old.

This is where the gratitude comes in. Your decision was based on many factors, and most of them are your own business. But the fact that your decision is known to me and to my children makes it our business. And I am grateful for that. I am thanking you first of all for refusing to serve as an Israeli soldier occupying the land of another people who desire their independence from us. I am also thanking you for sharing this decision with us, for inviting us to respond to your decision, to make this issue a matter of personal, family, and national debate.

Can it be right, or even necessary, for Israel's army to take up positions against a desperate Palestinian people, and to ruthlessly put down every spasm of resistance to our might and control? Have we been given sovereignty and the ability to choose our destiny only to deny these same rights to our closest neighbors?

With these questions, you open a window of truth for us all, no matter what our age or politics. Once we look through this window, none of us can avoid deciding for ourselves.

Thank you.
Henry R. Carse

NOVEMBER IN JERUSALEM
Jerusalem, 4th November 2000

On October 31st, the shooting reached the streets in my neighborhood in East Jerusalem. An Israeli guard at the local branch of the National Insurance Services was shot to death and another seriously wounded, assumedly by Palestinian gunmen, who got away. No one was terribly surprised.

On the evening of November 1st, I phoned Palestinian colleagues and heard confirmation that Israeli helicopters and tanks were bombarding homes in Beit Jala and El Khader, and that two more Palestinians were dead, presumably from Israeli fire. Meanwhile, a bomb, presumably planted by a Palestinian, went off in the heart of Israeli West Jerusalem, near the Jerusalem Theater, and people were injured. No one was terribly shocked.

On November 2nd, the radio announced that Arafat and Peres had agreed to a ceasefire. No one was terribly impressed. During the day shooting continued.

On November 3rd, Islamic Jihad terrorists detonated a car bomb in a market place in West Jerusalem, killing two Israelis. No one was terribly surprised.

Today, November 4th, is the anniversary of the assassination of Israel's Prime Minister Yitshak Rabin. No one, it seems, has anything but deep regrets.

Five bloody weeks have passed since the explosion of violence which some are calling the "New *Intifada*," some the "Al Aqsa *Intifada*," some the "Battle for Jerusalem." I don't know what to call it, but it is terrifying. The scenes of shooting, the bombardment of homes with tanks and missiles, the explosions, the lynchings. More people have been killed and wounded (reportedly over 150 dead and 6000 injured) in this one month than in the entire first year of the First Uprising of 1988.

But who cares?

Let's be honest. It's not easy for most folks elsewhere to pay any attention to what goes on in places with Arabic names like Kalandia and Jabaliya and El-Bireh and Beit Jala, or in places with Hebrew names like Gilo and Pisgat Ze'ev and Gush Etsion. Only if translated into "people we know" does the impact of so much mayhem begin to sink in.

Imagine, for example, that in one month 13,000 people die in the United States of gunshot wounds in civil strife, and a further 540,000 are injured. Imagine that. Or...never mind.

An old Israeli pop tune goes:

> *Four hundred million Chinese!*
> *I think about them...then I forget.*

It is a natural defense mechanism for our brains to turn off after the thousandth shooting, house demolition or lynching. The human system is not built for protracted disgust. To tell the truth, I am relieved when on some days the World News doesn't mention Israel and Palestine until at least five minutes into the program, which is to say, hardly at all.

I watch TV on my porch. I hear explosions and sirens from a few blocks away, but the announcer is highlighting airline crashes and floods. And why not? Doesn't someone else get a chance to be miserable? Perhaps it is not so terrible that the media attention on Jerusalem is waning. Do we really want the whole world to see images of us shooting and shouting at each other *ad nauseum*?

Who should really care? *We* should. And now is the time. Only the folks who live here can do the work, and it will help if the gawking crowds of uninvolved voyeurs let us shut the media window a bit and take a look at where we stand. Now is the right moment for the reawakening of the dialogue, wiser and more realistic, which will lead to peace. The media coverage has opened this conflict up to international discussion, which is important. We have been given enough images to convince us that both sides can be brutal. Now, we need to act on what we know. For that we need thought, prayer, healing, insight, and communication – not exposure. The folks with cameras can take a break and film floods for a while. You can't film soul-searching, especially the ugly kind.

Last Friday I joined Rabbis for Human Rights in a nonviolent demonstration at a busy street crossing in downtown West Jerusalem. The crossing was very small and it was filled with over a hundred people. Hardly a critical mass, but in these times better than nothing. Many of those present were veterans of the Women in Black group who have been protesting in that spot every Friday since 1967 – demanding an end to the Israeli Occupation of the Palestinian Territories. I rather shyly joined the demonstrators, standing on the sidewalk with my home-made sign reading *"The Occupation Must End!"* I found an elderly member of "Women in Black" eyeing me.

"Why are you here?" she asked.

"To tell you the truth, to make myself feel a bit better, less guilty for not being here years ago."

"That's what I thought. It's not enough."

Of course she is right – she has the daunting advantage of knowing what she is talking about. It is not enough to show up. What is needed is a gut-level understanding that the continued Occupation of the Palestinian Territories by Israel is one of this century's most grotesque mistakes.

We now know (unless we confine our reading to *US News & World Report*) that in the seven years since the vaunted Oslo Accords, the plight of Palestinians has worsened, not improved, and that Israelis are less secure, not more.

A month ago, a number of Palestinians, armed with guns and ammunition provided them under the Oslo agreements, got really and truly mad. They opened fire; right now it doesn't matter who was the first to pull the trigger. Palestinian gunmen tangled with Israeli military outposts on roads to Israeli settlements. The army responded, killing people who happened to be in the wrong place, as well as people who were shooting.

Palestinians shot at civilians living in Israeli settlements or hiking around in the territories. They opened fire from villages, shooting at settlement-suburbs on the outskirts of Jerusalem. Now they are driving by and shooting National Insurance employees and people out doing their Sabbath shopping. Post offices and banks are next, and malls and markets and all the rest. This is really happening.

Many Israelis who have considered themselves staunch supporters of Palestinian rights are shocked, stunned into angry silence or even into denunciation of the Palestinians as a whole. As a result, when Israeli helicopters rocket private homes every other night in retaliation, it seems that not a single Israeli blinks.

I can hear the justifications. "Oh, no! Israel is only responding directly to Palestinian fire!" Well, I just got off the phone with a friend in Beit Sahour whose house was hit three times in one night, her car smashed by a shell where it stood, while she and her parents and her young siblings cowered on the floor in panic. This is really happening.

When I first wrote "Dreams or Nightmares" on October 15th, I stated that the West Bank and the Gaza Strip must be declared a Palestinian State, and that Israeli settlements have to be dismantled, and that Jerusalem has to be shared. An American friend, who is also an occasional critic, read it and told me that my words would encourage the Islamic Jihad, and warned me not to mix politics with spirituality. After I cooled down a bit I amended my essay to read "most of the West Bank" and "most of the Israeli settlements." Now I wonder if that was cowardly. I doubt that people who support Islamic Jihad care what I wrote. As for those who are searching for peace, well, for them I devoutly wish that I could find stronger – not milder – terms for the horrors this Occupation is bringing on us. Is the truth less true when tempers are ablaze? Should "spiritual" folk hide their heads in platitudes and leave the strong language to militants?

Reactions to the call for compromise are harshest when the price of compromise is most obvious. As I stood at Paris Square on that Friday afternoon holding my simple (and much too mild) message about ending the Occupation, Israeli drivers slowed their cars to shout: "You consort with lynchers!," "You are insane!," "You are traitors!" Most impressive, however, were drivers who simply rolled down their windows and gave us the finger. This anger runs very deep, and it will not go away in a day or a month or a year. Israelis are angry that the *status quo* is being questioned, that the illusion of a "benign Israeli Occupation" is being exposed. Many feel bitterly betrayed and mocked, and that hurts.

Deep healing is needed, not blame, and this will take not only patience but an absolutely clear objective. That objective is peace, full peace in the arms of justice. Not a "unilateral separation" which promises Palestinians the prospect of isolated "*Palestans*" – a degrading local form of apartheid – while promising Israelis a permanent armed camp scenario. We don't need the "emotional" or "romantic" peace that lulled us in the past, the "*houmous and jalabiya*" peace of the culture mongers who thought it was cool to have a Palestinian friend or drink a Palestinian beer. We don't need the "peace" of Israeli liberals talking to themselves.

Real peace can only be realized between two very real enemies who are ready to compromise. We need Israeli peacemakers, and we need Palestinian peacemakers too. Where are they?

Yesterday I attended a meeting hosted by a Palestinian Christian organization dedicated to nonviolent resistance. The subject of discussion was a Christian response to the "New *Intifada*." There were only about twenty people there. Half were expatriates living temporarily in Jerusalem. The others were Palestinian Arab Christians who have been living under the Occupation for 33 years. One of these spoke of the "devastation" he felt at the silence of the Israeli peace camp. He added that we should not expect the Muslim and Jewish blocks of contestants in this bloody upheaval to put down their guns and "talk it over like good Christians." It was a pessimistic perspective. What, then, *can* we expect?

Can we even dream that mosques and synagogues of the Holy Land will preach nonviolence from their pulpits? Isn't it more likely that everyone will say: "Defend yourselves! Shoot back!" Isn't this the human, the logical, the reasonable response when you are shot at?

What happened twenty years ago, when a Palestinian peace activist launched a genuine nonviolent campaign, following guidelines inspired by Gandhi and King? Was he not immediately silenced, not only by the Israeli Army (surprise!) but – more shocking and more relevant – by the incumbent Palestinian Resistance Leadership, which regarded the nonviolent movement as a threat to its "armed struggle"?

How pleasant to dream of Palestinian and Israeli activists linking arms, singing an Arabic/Hebrew version of *"We Shall Overcome,"* to the admiring cheers of thousands of war-weary citizens, tears of joy streaming down their bearded cheeks! Get real. Every kind of nonviolent strategy has been aborted. Children are taught – by example and by decree – to pick up stones and hurl them. "Stone a soldier until he shoots you" appears to be the order of the day. If you have a better weapon, by all means use it. And – the clincher – if you can't find a soldier, just attack any Israeli you can find.

But wait a minute. Here is an Arab analyst writing an article asserting that the military option is misguided. He says (correctly enough) that there is no strategy in the use of arms in the Palestinian camp, that it is suicide for Palestinians with side-arms to shoot at Israelis with tanks and helicopters.

But what does this daring analyst suggest? Does he propose a strategic nonviolent campaign to win over the West – and Israel – at the precise moment when nonviolent action could end the Occupation by sheer force of conscience? Sadly, no. The "armed struggle" remains the sacred cow of Palestine, exactly as it was for Israel in its pre-state years. This analyst is merely saying: "Don't shoot now, get bigger guns!"

As for Israelis – well, the order of the day is the order of the last fifty years. Everyone knows that God gave Israel victory. Everyone knows that a gun is an Israeli cultural accessory, like a mobile phone. Everyone knows that the Occupation has to be upheld because politics has decreed it. Everyone knows that using one of the world's best-trained armies to protect illegal Jewish settlements is a national priority. In Israel, who cares if one lone soldier – obviously a "traitor" – refuses to serve in the Occupied Territories? Security is our moral imperative. Arabs are shooting, so we shoot back!

We have so long ignored the moral impact of the Occupation, and its cancerous effect on both Israeli and Palestinian society, that we now face a bloody amputation of precious limbs, a trauma that may cripple if not kill us. If we demand victory, if we reject compromise, there is no other way. Can anyone conceive of peace without victory? Is that an oxymoron?

When I arrived on the shores of this dear and benighted land in 1970, the air was full of the scent of victory. Israel's 1967 vanquishing of her Arab foes seemed so compelling that few doubted that it was an indication of moral excellence, if not outright divine intervention. Even Palestinians whose land was now occupied by Israel were heard to say that God must have willed it so. Maybe Jewish rulers would be more gracious than Jordanians or Egyptians.

Voices warned Israel not to keep the conquered land; they were ignored. Victory exuded euphoria. We all breathed deep, and we all bear some responsibility for the myth of the "Benign Occupation." All of us – occupiers, occupied, and suppliers of arms to both – have swallowed the sweet poison of victory and its twin sister, defeat. "What's yours is mine" is the rule of war. "Might makes right" means "winner takes all."

If the rule of war is the only rule, Palestinians should certainly get bigger guns. If "might makes right," Israelis should shoot back with a vengeance. God help us as this righteous war unfolds, with both sides celebrating the "rightfulness" of their convictions.

But what if victory does not equal morality? What if Israel's 1967 moment in history was not a divine intervention but superior firepower combined with the will to survive? Is this so impossible? Can't we now see that Palestinians too have their moment in history? That they too have a will to survive, that they are not going to disappear, and that they can even become Israel's partners in the future? Can't we see our way to peace without victory?

The message of Gandhi was *not* "beat your opponent without wasting bullets," nor "celebrate victory with a moral bonus of feeling good about yourself." The nonviolent methods developed by modern moral giants were based on strategies of radical restraint. They invoked the teachings of a Galilean Rabbi who refused to hate, even when hatred was the only logical response. The message of nonviolent action is only meaningful in the context of a nonviolent way of life – in other words, only when "spiritual" folk get their hands dirty.

Nonviolent options are viable when one knowingly renounces a significant part of what one knows to be one's by right. Why would anyone do that? Give the enemy more than he deserves? Give something up, knowing that one will receive absolutely nothing in return? Why on earth would anyone be so stupid?

What makes nonviolence the opposite of stupid is the paradox of human nature called *conscience*. Conscience is knowledge, not *naïveté*. Conscience, when awakened, has the power of pragmatism. Conscience knows that the enemy of today is tomorrow's business partner, that today's terrorist is tomorrow's diplomat, that today's hatred cannot outlast the need for tomorrow's friendship. The heart of the paradox is this: pragmatic nonviolence is also the only force that can awaken the conscience of my enemy.

Nowhere is this more true than in Jerusalem. In the midst of the shouting match about rights and the shooting match about land, I hear another voice. It is the voice of Israelis and Palestinians who would try the nonviolent way but lack only the knowledge of how it is done. Jerusalem is not ineligible for conscience. Nonviolence hastened the end of British Occupation in India, relief from brutal racial injustice in America, and the demise of apartheid in South Africa. It can work here too, but conscience is needed.

The aim of a nonviolent campaign in Israel and Palestine must be a consensus of support for one of the primary courses of action that will lead to peace: removal of Israeli settlements from the West Bank and Gaza. Here, in defiance of international law, thousands of Israeli civilians live. Regrettably, they have been misled to believe that it is okay to build villas on another people's farmland and fill swimming pools with another people's water.

Israel is trapped by its own defense of Jewish settlements beyond the boundaries of the State of Israel. Are settlers Jewish visionaries? Only if the vision sees Judaism as a suicidal zealotry or a modern Masada. Are they heroes of Zionism? Only if Zionism equals *"landolatry"*– the worship of divinely given territory – instead of democracy and justice. Only Israelis themselves can determine whether this is the Judaism and the Zionism they are prepared to live and die for. Meanwhile, persons of goodwill everywhere can support the nonviolent strategy.

This is a clear objective: the withdrawal of Israeli settlements and settlers from the Occupied Palestinian Territories. Every meter of withdrawal represents acres of agonizing over the "status of Jerusalem," the largest red herring in history. Unilateral withdrawal of settlements can be a form of elective surgery bringing long term healing and peace. And, just possibly, this can be done nonviolently; maintaining the Occupation most certainly cannot.

Nonviolent action is unattractive because it means admitting that I have been wrong, that the history I have written for myself and my cause is not the whole truth. Nonviolence is unattractive because it denies me the luxury of hating those who act hatefully, and the natural satisfaction of watching my enemy suffer.

Nonviolence in Israel and Palestine is not yet "strategic." It does not appear to meet the criterion of "most likely to succeed." Shooting seems more logical. However, the option is there, and it will not go away.

In Palestine and Israel, the peacemakers are gathering for a journey to sanity. The way of nonviolence is unpaved, and all the road signs point in the other direction. But we will not be alone on this path, and – in the long run – it is the only way we can rightly choose.

SOME BAD WIZARDS
Jerusalem, 23rd November 2000 – Thanksgiving Day

In 1900, L. Frank Baum published *The Wonderful Wizard of Oz*. What a tale of courage, compassion and wisdom! Over a billion people have watched the 1939 MGM film.

Unforgettable.

In the 1880s, this same L. Frank Baum wrote two editorials in his South Dakota newspaper, calling for the United States Army to come into the Dakotas, to defend the white settlers from the Native Americans, and to bring about the "total annihilation of the few remaining Indians."

Regrettable, but forgettable.

Psychic duality is the great mystery of human nature. Who was L. Frank Baum? A gentle daddy telling bedtime stories of soft wonder, or an advocate of genocide? Baum's sham wizard's words to Dorothy are revealing: "Oh no, my dear; I'm really a very good man; but I'm a very bad Wizard." Kindness and cruelty in one heart.

Recently the Israeli air force bombed Gaza, where over one million Palestinians live in the largest open-air prison on earth. Dozens were injured, including children. Less than twelve hours earlier, Palestinian terrorists attacked a bus full of kids near the settlement of Kfar Darom in Gaza, killing two and wounding nine (including five children, three of whom lost one or both their legs). Arafat says it wasn't his fault. Barak says it's not his fault Gaza got bombed. Neither of these leaders are bad men, but they have become very bad wizards.

In the seventies, I first met with some of the founders of *Gush Emunim*, an ideological settler movement which was to become one of the most radical groups to build Israeli settlements in the

West Bank and Gaza. Frankly, I thought they were great. They were young, intelligent, communicative; they had the courage of their convictions. I did not believe that they could hurt a flea, to say nothing of shooting at random into "troublesome" local equivalents of reservations, or cheerfully uprooting hundreds of ancient olive trees to provide a clear field of vision for their rifles, to protect their illegal settlements. They became bad wizards too.

One afternoon, in the halcyon days when we could actually visit the Holy Land without getting mauled, I was on a bus full of pilgrims driving through Nablus. We saw a gang of Palestinian kids swinging a puppy by a rope around its neck against a wall. When I rushed over and took the puppy away (she was still alive) I noticed two Palestinian policemen in uniform lounging nearby, watching and laughing. They could not understand what was bothering me; maybe their experiences in Israeli jails had numbed them. Bad wizards in uniform.

I don't understand how a cute and sassy 19-year-old Israeli guy can be the kind of sniper who (as statistics now show) always aims for the genitals of young Palestinian demonstrators. I don't understand how an Israeli helicopter pilot, who shot missiles into residential Jericho, can say: "Once I've received my target, it all becomes technical. I look at the target sheet and see that our target is a school... I'm ashamed that I did not ask about the exact nature of our target, but not that I attacked it... There's no alternative." Bad wizards feeling bad.

I don't get it. I don't understand how a Palestinian detonating a large explosive device by the roadside can wait until a school bus filled with Israeli kids is exactly in range before closing the circuit.

I don't understand how the people of the USA can mandate their government to broker peace, and then watch apparently unmoved as Israeli pilots with US ammunition launch projectiles through the walls of civilian homes in Beit Sahour where children are cowering on the floor. I don't get how supporters of the "struggle for freedom" can condone a Palestinian bomber who detonates a car bomb in the heart of Hadera, destroying a bus full of tourists and white-haired Jewish ladies in their sixties.

I don't understand how the Palestinian Authority can glorify with a martyr's title 12-year-olds who throw themselves against Israeli tanks with rocks in their hands, and then neglect to provide psychologists or social workers to talk with Palestinians suffering from post-traumatic stress. I don't understand it when people in clear distress tell me that only foreign aid workers and journalists care about their pain.

If I am baffled by all this, why am I not baffled by myself?

In the morning I can cross the lines to visit a 55-year-old man who sits crying by the ruins of his house in Beit Jala; the same evening I can sit at home eating ice cream. With the *sang-froid* of a concentration camp commandant, I watch on TV the latest scenes of a wounded girl screaming and thrashing in the emergency room of the Gaza hospital, or graphic shots of bloodstains from the latest bus bombing in Jerusalem.

I am baffled and frightened by all of this because I do not understand my own heart and its deceits. I, too, am L. Frank Baum.

We are all caught between Oz and Gaza, between our apathy and our compassion. We are good people but, God help us, very bad wizards. We manipulate our audiences with loud noises and bogus power, while we fear exposure and crave affection. We are stranded in a dangerous dream-land far from home, caught in a fantasy of our own making which we believe to be a magical creation. When, like Dorothy from Kansas, innocence appears in our fortresses, all we can do is play our power games and stay behind our curtain, swaggering and bullying our way through the next crisis, hoping that Toto doesn't discover how pathetic our magic really is.

Wizardry is bad policy. This is why I believe, even now, that the nonviolent option is the only way for Israel and Palestine. Whatever the caliber of my weapon, if I am shooting the "other," I am forced to deny that the "other" is like myself. I can only kill from a desperate position, a position behind a veil, from which I cannot afford to see the human beauty and uniqueness I am destroying. This is true whether I am detonating a powerful explosive from 100 meters away to rip through a busload of children, or launching the missile that shatters the body of the doctor on his way to care for a neighbor. The rock in the hand and the high-velocity projectile in the gunbarrel are unalike in strategic weight, but they are identical in the fear and desperation, the bluster and the numbness they represent. It's all bad magic, bad medicine, and it is turning us to stone.

"I will take away your heart of stone, and give you a human heart." This phrase from the prophets is not only the best theology and the best psychology ever written, but the best guideline for the freedom struggle as well. A "human heart" is the only change radical enough to have radical (not just reactionary) consequences and to open the road to peace.

So...if there is anyone who might still be listening, back there in the Kansas of normal life, please know this. Each one of us in Jerusalem and in her "daughters" – Ramallah, Bethlehem, Beit Sahour, Pisgat Zeev and Gilo – each one of us has a heart of stone. This is why the things we do in this tornado-induced nightmare seem strange and heartless – because they are. We have straw for brains, and we swagger when we should be brave. We follow the yellow brick road and discover only the divided house of our own self-conceit. Brainless, spineless and heartless, we expect our local bad wizards to get us home. They will fail us, and save only their own skins. At best, we learn from Toto to rip aside the curtain, to reveal the deceit behind the scenes. At worst, we fall into the clutches of the witchery of ultra-nationalism and ethnic cleansing that lies ahead.

So please, all you folks back there in Kansas, if you still love the shadows of yourselves trapped here in Oz, then please hear this. Do not send us your better weapons, projectiles clearly marked "Made in USA." Do not send us your advisors to tell us how to subdue our enemies or to outwit those more desperate than we are. Do not send us eloquent prayers for Jews or Arabs in distress, or money to build more roads and settlements, or to arm the next militia.

Send us only someone to break our hearts of stone.

CAGES
Hebron, 10th December 2000

Hebron. *El-Khalil. Hevron.* The ancient city of Abraham, called "God's friend." An enigma of biblical proportions; a puzzle of mythical significance; a human trap of the direst kind. If I had the combined writing talent of Kafka and Rushdie, the combined artistic eye of Blake and Bacon, the combined human insight of Tich Nhat Hanh and a shaman sitting in the fire, I would still be unable to describe Hebron under Israeli Occupation at the dawn of the 21st century: desperate, possessed, twisted, broken, caged.

A group of foreign ex-pats and internationals (locally dubbed "intees") organize to visit Hebron, to observe the situation in the Israeli Occupied area of the city (known laconically as H2) and to express support for the Palestinian community living there under difficult conditions.

Bright blue sky and startling winter sunshine cover red rocky earth and terraced hillsides, and grapevines stand shoulder high, crowned with yellow winter leaves. The road to Hebron winds past Bethlehem into a countryside older than Abraham. Our bus is loaded with "intees" of every ilk – NGO and aid workers, fact finders, human rights activists, journalists. I am suddenly thinking of my sister's tales of her journey to Selma, Alabama in the sixties…"To be where justice is not."

At a checkpoint we are turned back. A long line of service taxis and a huge crowd of Palestinian workers trying to get to work show that there is an *ad hoc* Israeli Army roadblock, so we turn toward the longer bypass road and head East, coming at Hebron from the other side.

The organizers, using the bus microphone, give us a fine briefing. They remind us that we are an informal international presence. We have come to observe and to demonstrate a supportive role; this is not an intervention. Many in the group must retain their visa status with the Israeli authorities, so confrontation with Israeli settlers or the army is not the intention of this journey. Our presence is the important thing.

Contact persons are designated, mobile phone numbers are written down, and soon we are in Hebron. We park in sight of the Ibrahimi Mosque, that mysterious monument to the ancestor of us all. As we gaze at the massive tomb structure with its crenellated wall, we see Muslim men going in to pray after being stopped and searched by the Israeli soldiers on duty. Here, as Genesis tells it, Abraham purchased a cave to bury his wife Sarah. Later, he too was to rest there beside her, and the tombs of Isaac, Jacob, Rebecca and Leah are close at hand. Are they restless in their tombs, these patriarchs and matriarchs, curfewed and closured and caged?

We are on our way into Hebron. Moving first through the Palestinian part of the city (known as H1), we gather at Bab Ez-Zaweyeh Square, and are joined by Christian Peacemaking Team members, who will be our guides. The curfew has been lifted until 1 p.m., so we have some time to visit.

We move into H2, passing checkpoints under the quizzical looks of the Israeli soldiers, and reach a building called Beit Hadassa. This has been a focus of Israeli presence ever since Rabbi Moshe Levinger and his pioneer settlers arrived in 1968. Everywhere are distinctive signs of Jewish history in Hebron. Stars of David carved on old buildings are reminders that here the Jewish community remembers its roots from at least the 16th century. More modern Jewish story in Hebron is sandwiched uncomfortably between the Arab massacre of 60 Jews in Hebron in 1929 (400 other Jews were protected and saved by their Arab neighbors), and the more recent massacre of 29 Arabs by the Jewish settler Dr. Baruch Goldstein in 1994 (no other Jews were around to intervene).

A sickening aura of religious and ethnic desperation in this city casts the interfacing of Arab and Jew in a context of unmitigated trauma. In 1997, after the 1995 Oslo II agreements, Israeli forces withdrew from around 80% of the city; that part became H1, under Palestinian "autonomous control." The remaining 20% became H2, under Israeli Army Occupation.

H2 is a web of impossibilities. It encompasses the Ibrahimi Mosque, the old Arab market (the *Qasbah*) and Palestinian dwellings adjacent to those of Israeli settlers. Jewish and Arab homes are right on top of each other, interlaced with barbed wire, gargantuan protective shields, sniper crow's nests, barricades of concrete-filled barrels, no-go zones, army camps, sand-bagged synagogues and *yeshiva* study halls. Day and night, over a thousand Israeli soldiers are stationed in H2 to protect the 500 Jewish settlers from their Arab neighbors, and – ostensibly – to protect Arab residents from hostile settler activity.

Implementing the Israeli Occupation in Hebron challenges reason. Back in the 1980s a CBS special report covered the conflict in Israel and Palestine, and the commentator said (the phrase has stayed with me, resonating with the dark humor of truth): "This is where creative disgrace has been elevated to an art form." In Hebron, "creative disgrace" flourishes.

Take curfew for instance. When we arrive, H2 has been under sporadic curfew for 70 days. However, the curfew applies only to Palestinian residents, not Jews. Goods and services are not allowed into Palestinian areas. Reportedly, 40,000 Palestinians have fled their homes to escape the choke-hold of checkpoints, harassment, auto and body searches, and the seizure of private homes by both the army and Israeli settlers.

We visit the Cordova Girls' School, perched just above Beit Hadassa. The headmistress, Firyal, greets us, and some of the 180 students give us the school song – it is about the fight for freedom – an *ad hoc* civics lesson. There have been two days of studies at Cordova in the last two months; the rest of the time, curfew. During curfew, many of Hebron's Arab schools are closed, and 12,000 students have no access. Most of the syllabus will not be taught this year, but local Palestinian TV stations are broadcasting lessons so children under curfew can do some catching up. Illiterate parents are tuning in as well. The curfew has made learning a family matter.

Meanwhile, the army has occupied three school buildings and a school playground for use as military posts. At the Cordova Girls' School, settlers have been hanging Israeli flags on the fence, harassing the children as they come to school, and – "Oh, yes," says Firyal, "I have video of night raids by settlers into the school grounds."

"Night raids?"

We move on, into the market streets. We visit the Sherabati family's home in the heart of old Hebron. As we duck into the low doorway, we see concrete Israeli settlement structures looming above us, barbed wire enclosing occupied rooftops like a lethal stage setting for a *Diehard* action thriller, army bunkers on metal scaffolding with 500mm machine guns protruding, water tanks the size of grain silos with giant blue and white Israeli flags painted on them.

Shahnaz Sherabati greets us in her handkerchief-sized and spotless flag-stoned patio, colorfully decorated with flowering cactus plants and geraniums. The homey effect is marred jarringly by the fact that the entire patio is caged in, sealed with a protection shield of heavy wire meshing. This was put up by the Sherabati family to block incoming volleys of cement blocks, glass bottles, used disposable diapers, discarded plastic kitchen utensils, twisted pieces of metal, and eggs and paint, all from the Jewish settlement building above them.

The wire mesh stops everything but the eggs and paint, which make heavy smears on the whitewashed wall. The rest of the stuff is lodged up there on the meshing, in thickening haphazard layers, between the Sherabati family and the light of day.

"In 1982 it began," says Shahnaz. Her voice is very quiet, level, cheerful. Two of her nieces and a nephew stand with her at the house door, giggling to get their picture taken. "The Jewish settlers damaged our home then and put up their settlement building right above us. My father was still alive then. We had lots of trouble from the settlers. They began yelling day and night and throwing things. Ever since then they have been, well...bad neighbors, I am sorry to say.

They took away sheets of roofing we had up over the patio, exposing us. They threw stones, garbage, eggs and paint. The Jewish policemen came to try to work something out, but all efforts amounted to nothing.

We have daily problems, I can say. Those settlers hope to force us out, now that my father is gone. They thought that we would leave when he died. But we will not leave, ever.

A little over a year ago we put up this metal cage to protect ourselves. The settlers cut our telephone line. They shout and say bad things, when the children are in the yard, and throw things, but *Nushkur Allah*, no one has been hurt!

The children? They don't pay them any attention! There are six of us here now, since my father died, and sometimes my brothers come over when we are having a bad time. We often need to call the Temporary International Presence in Hebron, and even the Israeli police. I am a staff nurse at the Government Hospital in H1. With great effort I am able to make it to work in spite of everything, *Nushkur Allah!*"

We take our leave. "*Allah ya'atiki el affiyeh.*" Outside, near the *Qasbah*, the returning curfew in H2 tightens gradually, like a giant clam closing its shell under a stormy sea. Soldiers station themselves at key junctures. A big settler Volvo cruises by, with dark windows. I can glimpse young faces, a woman's headscarf, a man with a beard. It sports a bumper sticker in Hebrew: "*Milhama Achsav* – War Now."

Carloads of skull-capped youths drive up and park near the east end of the market. Settlers on foot with guns slung over their shoulders saunter among the soldiers. The square at the *Qasbah*'s east end becomes a stage upon which a series of surreal, loosely connected scenes will be enacted. It is the curfew ritual. We stand with the Palestinian workers and shop owners just inside the market entrance, observing and photographing. The players know their parts.

From the alley behind us, a Palestinian man comes out of the *Qasbah*, pushing a hand-cart filled with tattered plastic bags and some old dirty pails. He trundles past us and comes up against a line of soldiers in full battle gear, flak jackets and helmets, with sound- and smoke-grenades clipped to their lapels and short-stocked M16's tucked up tight under their chins. One of the soldiers directly blocks the path. A dialogue ensues.

Soldier: "Hold it! What's this stuff?"
Palestinian: "It's garbage I'm bringing over to that dumpster over there."
Soldier: "Who'd you say is garbage?"
Palestinian: "I didn't say anyone is garbage. This is garbage."
Soldier: "So you think I'm garbage?"
Palestinian bystanders: "Not you! He's talking about the garbage he's dumping!"
Soldier: "You'd like to dump me?"
Palestinian: "What's with you? I'm just trying to dump some garbage!"
Second Soldier (coming onstage left): "Hey, what's going on?"
First Soldier: "This guy is calling me garbage."
Second Soldier: "What makes him think you like being called garbage?"

And so forth. Meanwhile the soldiers have orders from the officer in charge. They press all the Palestinians back into the entrance to the market, and we move with them, standing among them with our cameras, our jeans and jackets and red baseball caps and cowboy boots and other unmistakable international stuff.

It is getting crowded. We are now all standing behind a makeshift army barricade of metal produce tables. Some of the Palestinians head off toward the Palestinian area of H1 behind us. There will be no more business today, and they hope to get home before hostility breaks out. Others need to get through the square in front of us, going to their homes in H2. But this means passing the soldiers and walking through the settlers who are now gathering *en masse*. It is not yet one o'clock, but the curfew is closer. Palestinians out on the street during a curfew can be shot, while Israeli settlers can move around freely.

Lanky settler guys in white shirts, with handguns stuck into their pants at the back, are arguing with the police. There is a heated altercation. One of the settlers is knocked down by a police officer. He is staying down, breathing heavily, being treated by an army medic. An ambulance stands by, although not needed, yet.

A few Palestinian men and women are approaching from the east, moving across the square toward the *Qasbah* and the relative safety of H1. Soldiers and settlers now form something like a loose net, an armed sieve stretching right across the square. It is fifteen minutes before one. The curfew should not be in force yet. The Palestinians keep walking through the sieve. A settler lurches forward, catches a Palestinian man with his shoulder. The Palestinian stumbles, catches his balance and, looking straight ahead, keeps walking.

Nearer to where we stand, a tall, elegant and somewhat mysterious Palestinian man comes out of the market, wearing a long woolen robe decorated with neat triangular red patches. He has steady eyes, a square face, a neatly trimmed beard. He walks right up to the "Am I Garbage?" soldier.

"Excuse me, but my house is over there" (pointing across the square)… "Can I go over to my house?" His voice is high, raspy, comical, as if he might have inhaled a bit of helium along the way, or (more likely under the circumstances) as if he has suffered a recent throat injury. He stands there, oddly still, looking at the soldier, as settlers mill around and the "intees" take pictures.

Am-I-Garbage looks Bearded Man up and down. He holds his M16 at the ready, just in case Bearded Man should decide to detonate some plastic explosives and blow them both into little fragments. Am-I-Garbage raises his eyebrows. A new look crosses his face, an amused leer.

"Hey! Come over here, you guys!" Two other soldiers move his way, stepping sideways around the crowd of Palestinians, like crabs in an aquarium moving around a bed of sea urchins.
"Listen to this," says Am-I-Garbage. "You won't believe this, you gotta hear this!"

Bearded Man speaks again, asking permission to go home, in the same squeaky voice, but with great dignity. The soldiers listen raptly, then chortle, shake their heads and walk away.

"No way, buddy," says Am-I-Garbage flatly. "Curfew's on."
It is five minutes before one o'clock.

A dozen young Jewish settler women arrive in the square. They eye the crowd of Palestinians jammed behind the metal table barricade in the shadowy market. The square is secure, the stage clear, so they walk on, arm in arm, giggling. The young women, dressed in modest skirts and buttoned-up blouses and sturdy shoes, their hair tied back, appear to be in their teens. They walk among the soldiers as some of the international press take pictures.

Suddenly, one of the young women whips out a large plastic bottle full of water and lunges in the direction of one of the photographers, a woman from Italy, who retreats behind a closed market stall. Simultaneously, another teenager pulls out an identical bottle and assaults another photographer, drenching both him and his camera. The Palestinians behind the tables surge forward slightly, with a collective "Whoa!" – like a Greek chorus in a tragic-comic production. Soldiers move half-heartedly after the settler girls to restrain them, but it is all over. The photographers retreat to the relative safety of the market, the settlers saunter off, victorious smiles wreathing their faces. It's all part of the curfew game.

The plot-less H2 play is drawing to a close. The slanting light of a winter afternoon touches old stone and new concrete, the garbage in the street and the immense Israeli flags on the rooftops, with an incongruous beauty.

We stand in the now deserted market, about to leave the contrived tableaux of soldier/settler occupation of H2 to enter the Palestinian streets of H1. The "intees" are thoughtful, subdued. A young NGO volunteer shakes his head, bemused. "My God!" he mutters. "It's the most expensive baby-sitting job in history!"

The square at the eastern end of the *Qasbah* is now entirely in the hands of Jewish army and Jewish settlers, entirely Arab-free. In the square I glimpse, just as I turn away, three mature Jewish women in modest attire, hair covered, one of them pushing a stroller. From where I stand, I cannot tell if there is a child in the stroller. The group is remarkable for its casual intentionality: it's just an afternoon stroll by the Hebron *Qasbah* full of caged Arabs at curfew time.

Two of the women with the stroller are in earnest conversation. They might be, in another world, two contemplatives walking in a cloister. The third woman walks slightly to one side, resolute and protective, hefting in her right hand a two-foot wooden cudgel, which she is whacking rhythmically into her left palm. She says not a word, but I am reading her body language well: "Don't mess with me. I'm Jewish, I'm a woman, I'm a mother. I don't like Arabs, and I am here to stay."

This woman's irrefutable gestures are clear to me, but I can't quite see her eyes. As I turn away, moving out of one cage and into another, I wonder, for a brief instant, what those eyes might reveal. Then, with an inexplicable but unmistakable sense of shame, I realize that I do not want to know.

NO-ONE LAND
Jerusalem, 25th January 2001

Today I took a morning walk through No-One Land. This is not difficult, as I live in East Jerusalem, just a few paces from the former Mandelbaum Gate. My neighborhood in fact was known as "No Man's Land" from 1948 to 1967. Today, of course, nothing remains of the wall that divided Jerusalem all those years. A six-lane highway now roars along the "Green Line," with Palestinian East Jerusalem on one side and Israeli West Jerusalem on the other.

I have just returned from a Christmas vacation with family in the States. Images of tinseled trees in snowy Vermont are still dancing in my brain. Time for a morning walk around the block, time for a reality-check in No-One Land.

It is a beautiful sunny dawn after a soft night rain. The golden stones of Jerusalem are washed clean, and four-foot piles of garbage on the sidewalk (municipal workers' strike) don't smell a bit in the cool air. The mating cats that were screaming all night in the parking lot of the Ministry of Justice are apparently tuckered out. The young woman standing guard with her compact Uzi at the District Courthouse is yawning and sipping a cup of steaming *nescafé*. A few meters further on, a five-man IDF patrol is mustering in front of the derelict Alhambra Cinema; they click the firing bolts of their M16's in unison to check the chambers, and move off toward the Old City.

I walk north on Salladin Street as dozens of Ford mini-vans rush south, inches from my shoulder. They are packed with Palestinians coming in from Ramallah and El-Bireh and other communities in the Occupied West Bank. Their faces peer out of the windows, drawn and tired; they have been traveling since the dark hours to get around the army checkpoints. The drivers screech to a halt in the middle of the street on the corner. Women with babies in their arms, young men with checkered *keffiyehs*, older men in ancient tweed jackets, smartly dressed ladies in heels and *hijab*, with sharp make-up and briefcases, all pile out and dodge traffic, moving on to their workplaces.

The air is still fresh at the beginning of a new day. An IDF patrol jeep cruises past me, with six Druze soldiers wearing the dark olive uniforms and green berets of the hated Border Patrol, moving against traffic on the wrong side of the road, blasting nerve-jarring commands in "Hebaric" from the bull-horn screwed to the jeep's hood:

> *Ya'allah!* Out of the Way! Ford Escort – Pull Over!
> You – Yes, You! Peugeot Pick-Up – Back Up! Out
> of the Way! *Zoozoo Kvar Ya Zalameh!* Honk! Honk!
> BAGI IRAAGHRAA!

It is an indescribably invasive, corrosive din. Folks on the sidewalk don't miss a step: children with schoolbags, mothers with blanket-wrapped infants, guys selling sesame-seed cakes, arm-linked teenage girls in school uniforms – not one of them flinches as the jeep blares at them. They look the other way, faces impassive.

At the point where Nablus Road meets Salladin Street is the United Nations Relief Agency building. It's a nice old three-storey Arab-style stone residence-turned-anomaly, flying the blue and white UN flag. A lone white car sits in the yard. There is no movement, no sign of life. The flag marks a fantasy island in a gritty urban triangle, with Highway One on one side, a huge construction crater on the other, a massive Israeli-owned hotel on the third. Nearby, Palestinian parents are letting off their children in front of St. George's School. Ford vans try to squeeze by without slowing down. A big ramshackle interurban bus swerves up onto the sidewalk. Chaos. Traffic jam.

I turn and walk past the hotel, closed and deserted because no tourists in their right minds would buy a ticket to Jerusalem when the US State Department has a travel warning out about "violent clashes and confrontations." An exhausted cat is soaking up the early sun in the curve of the hotel driveway.

I cross Highway One, carefully, waiting a long time to find a crack in the traffic flow. There is no marked pedestrian crossing on Highway One. At rush hour it seems as impassable as a wall. Not, however, impassable for the nimble, nor for the desperate. This whole section of the highway, from the National Police Headquarters to Damascus Gate, is flowing with Palestinian day laborers filtering across traffic into West Jerusalem. They are on their way – illegally – to look for work.

Back at home, in the villages of the West Bank, tens of thousands are unemployed; families are living on homegrown tomatoes and borrowed flour. So, each morning, these men, a silent army of desperate wage-earners, cross Highway One against the flow of traffic, pretending to be invisible, hoping they will not be stopped by a policeman or patrolling soldier on the other side. They don't have permits, but they are determined. They hope for a day of labor in construction or street-sweeping, hope to go home with ten dollars minus the Ford mini-van fare, hope to disappear uncaught into the seething anonymity of the West Bank hinterlands, hope to repeat the odyssey tomorrow.

I cross through No-One Land with them. They look the other way, do not catch my eye. Across the highway, we are in West Jerusalem. Here, on the other side, is the ultra-orthodox Mea She'arim neighborhood. Modestly dressed Jewish women scurry up the sidewalk, and children in groups are off to school, girls with long braids and boys with *yarmulkes* perched on their heads. They ignore the clusters of Palestinian workers in rough dark clothes gathering in small groups at the street corners, waiting, like so many garden rakes stacked against a wall, for Israeli employers to cruise by in pick-up trucks and take them off to the building sites of Israel's urban growth.

The Palestinians know that they will be put to work building Israeli settlements. They will be trucked into their own land, now confiscated, fenced off and electronically protected. They will be transported, as if they were foreigners, to the sprawling suburbs on occupied land east of the city, to pour concrete, lay tiles, decorate and polish and beautify the *faux*-marble floors of villas in colonies where only Jews may live. They will engineer the permanence of the Occupation, in return for a few shekels from the contractors, a pat on the back and a word of thanks in Arabic: "*Shukran, habibi.* Good work, Musa. Off you go, then. See you next week, *Insha'allah.*"

Palestinians. Israelis. The invisible wall that thickens with each day between them is torn and punctured, ripped by a thousand little transgressions, then by night it seals again. They are locked in a dance of dependence; friendships and hatreds develop and fade. Comrades while they work, enemies while they sleep.

Israeli restaurant owners from Tel Aviv go shopping in a West Bank town, and are shot dead by militants in the local café. The army roadblocks are drawn tighter. Close the net, seal the membrane, choke the villages. A woman in labor tries to get through a checkpoint to the hospital. She is turned back by the soldiers, the baby dies. So, angry resistance taughtens, sharpens. Rip the net, shoot at passing cars, bomb the buses. And so forth.

It is all written in their eyes in the clear morning light, in Jerusalem, crossing Highway One. But you would have to lie down on your back on the street and gaze intently upward to get a glimpse of those eyes. They are downcast, hidden. The workers' wounded selves are wrapped in their tense bodies as they move across No-One Land.

I walk along a quiet side street past the Vatican's Notre Dame Center with its gold and white banner waving peacefully in the breeze. In the shadow of the Jerusalem Municipality building, with its blue and white Israeli flag, a street-sweeper is pushing his broom. I remember how in that very street I discovered the truth about Jerusalem street-sweepers.

It was a dark evening in 1972, the alley a lot dirtier and scarier than it is today. I was hurrying by on Jaffa Road, glanced into the shadows, and saw a street-sweeper pushing a wheeled bin of garbage. He wore no uniform and was squat, generic, unremarkable, his face invisible. As I looked, he reached into the garbage bin, drew out a crumpled Coke can and gravely began to talk into it. Then, holding it to his ear, he listened, nodding discreetly. I moved on. I never forgot.

This morning, years later, I catch this other street-sweeper's eye. He wears a municipal worker's vest, but his face says nothing. I want to speak, to break the spell of silence, to ask him what he is seeing, hearing, understanding. Suddenly I am confused, uncertain. I just don't know who he is – I can't tell if he is a Palestinian or a Jew, if he speaks Arabic or Hebrew or (increasingly likely) Russian. It is a hilarious moment. He pauses politely, gazing at me, wondering what on earth I want.

I turn back eastward and walk along the walls of the Old City. The 16th century ramparts soar above me to their crenellated tops, stones that have looked down into No-One Land for silent years and still tell nothing.

Poets speak what stones can't tell. Yehuda Amichai's prose poem comes to my mind, with its teasing tone:

> Once I sat on the steps by a gate at David's Tower;
> I placed my two heavy baskets at my side. A group
> of tourists was standing around their guide and I
> became their target-marker.
> "You see that man with his baskets? Just right of
> his head there's an arch from the Roman period. Just
> right of his head."
> "But he's moving, he's moving!"
> I said to myself, redemption will come only if
> their guide tells them, "You see that arch from the
> Roman period? It's not important. But next to it, left
> and down a bit, there sits a man who's bought fruit

and vegetables for his family."

It is all here: the walls, the gates, the man with his baskets, the woman with her pile of grape leaves, passers-by. But, today, no guide, no tourists. I look at the faces, Palestinian faces, of every person on that path below Jerusalem's silent wall. The faces do not say, "Redemption will come." They say, "We will stay, when tourists leave. We will stay, when invaders leave. You will leave. We will stay." Even the rumble and belch of raucous traffic pummeling down Highway One cannot mask the roar of these faces.

I move slightly away from the highway as it curves north from Damascus Gate. I am on the oriental edge of No-One Land. Workers and merchants gather, drink a strong *kahaweh arabiye*, pick up a sesame roll and a *felafel*. They squat smoking on rickety stools on the sidewalk, or they lean, chatting, against their trucks, colorfully decorated with *hamzas* and Qur'anic verses.

Here, at the edge of No-One Land, the muted are suddenly gregarious. The warm oily presence of the trucks, the comfort of numbers, the scent of cardamom, the knowledge that not so long ago this very sidewalk was in Jordan; something makes them smile at me as I walk by.

> *"Sabah el-kher! Ahallan Wa-sahallan!"*
> "Hey! Got any work for us today?"
> "Want some coffee? T-shirts? Taxi?"

Maybe I am a lost Anglo-Israeli contractor, or maybe a lone Irish tourist, or perhaps an *Intifada*-hungry journalist on the prowl. Whatever. Older men chuckle, faces cracking into a million wrinkles. A few younger men glare. But we are here, and our eyes meet, with questions for each other.

As I pass the Old Arab Bus Station I see someone has put up a smart new municipal sign – *"To the Jitney Station"* – as if a British High Commissioner or UN clerk is still drawing the maps in

Occupied Palestine. Here there is a veritable beehive of minivans, swerving and honking and generally swarming around, hardly slowing to disgorge passengers. At the corner of Nablus Road is the office of Israel's Interior Ministry, on the third floor of a nondescript mandate-period building, its entrance entirely caged in by a thick black metal mesh, with a seven-foot high turnstile. A couple of Israeli policemen stand inside while Palestinians wait on the sidewalk for the privilege of being allowed in to update their papers, hoping to hang on to a shred of identity for themselves.

I am just a few minutes now from home. The barber shop on the corner sports its eye-popping sign reading *The Golden Saloon*. Next door is the *High Life Grocery*. Both are still closed, it is early yet. Not only that, no one is eager to open for business today, because of yesterday's bombing.

Yesterday evening, just after six o'clock, we heard the big thumping roar of a bomb going off right near here, and then the predictable wail of sirens. The seven o'clock radio news didn't mention it, so we guessed that there had been no casualties. The morning paper, though, had something in the bottom corner of the front page about a "small detonation" near a hardware store.

Sure enough, here, around the corner from the Interior Ministry, is the hardware store, with a big hole in the sidewalk near the smoke-stained closed-tight metal door shutters. A parked Peugeot is missing its side windows, and the rear windshield seems to have come loose and is sliding down over the trunk. At the Jerusalem Hotel, windows are in smithereens, and an employee is sweeping up the glass among the potted plants. The framing store next door is the only place open. The owner is sitting at his desk, doing paper work.

"*Sabah el-kher. Ahallan Wa-sahallan.*"
"Sorry to see the damage from the bomb. Any idea what happened?"
"No, of course not. I wasn't here, you see."

"You are okay? Nobody hurt, I guess?"

"Well, as far as I know, I am okay. I'm not sure, of course, but I seem to be okay. What do you think?"

I am beginning to wonder about this conversation.

"Quite a lot of windows broken next door. I hope your shop is unharmed?"

"Yes, of course. You see, I sell glass here. So naturally nothing got broken."

I say goodbye and make my exit, feeling like an amateur actor in an Ibsen play.

The line of Palestinians at the Interior Ministry is already three times as long, and the people there look tired; some of them came at two in the morning to be sure to get in today, not next month. Back on Saladdin Street, the Border Patrol jeep is squarely occupying the sidewalk, so the pedestrians are walking in the street. One of the soldiers is stopping young men to check their ID cards.

There is, I notice, a new bread shop on Saladdin Street – *The French Crust*. I step in to congratulate the enterprising owners and to wish them luck.

"Congratulations! *Mabruk! Ya'atiku il-A'fiyeh!*"

"Thank you! May Heaven preserve your health!"

The aroma of freshly baked Palestinian *croissant* wafts into No-One Land. What do you know? I'm home.

GET THE CONNECTION
Jerusalem, 16th February 2001

On the day after Valentine's Day, the *Voice of Israel* news broadcast from Jerusalem was particularly poignant. A professor from Haifa University, on his way to a job interview in Kalamazoo, Michigan, got into trouble with security officers at Chicago airport; he told them he had a bomb and they were not amused. I guess he did not get the job.

An apparently unrelated news item from Kansas was about teaching evolution in public schools, and yet another told that experts say that asthma can be transmitted to infants through their mothers' milk.

In light of the current events of Valentine's Day in the Holy Land, however, the most relevant item was a report from a Californian psychologist who has found that Samson (the biblical Israelite hero who killed Philistines in Gaza with a jawbone) can be diagnosed as having an antisocial personality disorder.

This explains everything.

On Valentine's Day, a Palestinian bus driver by the name of Khalil was on duty with an Israeli bus company, *Egged*. Khalil was driving an empty bus toward Tel Aviv when he apparently made a sudden U-turn and headed south in the general direction of Gaza. *En route*, he plowed the bus into a crowd of soldiers and civilians waiting at a bus stop. Seven young soldiers and one civilian were killed, 26 others badly wounded.

The driver of the bus was a 35-year-old father of five, a "simple man, who never spoke violently," as his neighbor said to reporters. Khalil was in fact from Gaza, but had been cleared by security to work at Israel's largest bus franchise. He may never have spoken violently, but his way of observing Valentine's Day was to drive his bus into a human crowd.

"He acted out his love for his homeland," explained his brother, "...after he saw what Israel is doing to the Palestinians."

The Israeli victims' faces look gravely out at me from the front page of *Haaretz*. The men – Alexander (18), David (20), and Ophir (20). The women – Kokhava (19), Rachel (20), Yasmin (19), Simcha (30), and Julie (21). Julie was a new immigrant, from France; her parents will have to fly in for the funeral. All were soldiers except Simcha; she was just on her way to work. Look at them. Faces both beautiful and precious.

Something bothers me, through the sadness, about the photos. On a hunch, I quickly flip through the twelve pages of Israel's oldest and most liberal newspaper. Besides those eight faces, lots of people got in the paper that day: police, ambulance workers, mourning comrades, Israeli diplomats at the White House, orthodox Jews posing with Israeli soldiers, lawmakers, computer whiz kids, Israeli actors, and even an Israeli soccer star. Who is missing?

Not a single photograph of a Palestinian face. This must be just a coincidence; after all, the news today is the death of Israelis. Still...I look again.

Here we are, on page 3 – almost missed it. The funeral of Masoud Ayad, targeted from an Israeli helicopter gunship two days ago. Palestinian mourners, generic uniforms, a body wrapped in a Palestinian flag, a few distant dour faces. "Ayad, killed [sic] by Israeli gunships...was given a military funeral...and deemed a holy saint." Under the single photo of Ayad's funeral, a report of another assassination ("killing") of a Palestinian policeman in Tulkarem. "The Israel Defense Forces deny," writes the reporter, "that this was a planned attack."

Not a planned attack?

An Israeli professor, an expert on extremism, was recently interviewed on Israeli TV's *Channel 7*:

Interviewer: "What do you think about the executions in the Palestinian Authority?"

Professor S.: "I have a very positive opinion. I mean, it is a vital instrument, part of the struggle against terrorism and I have no reservation – "

Interviewer: "One moment, one moment. I was referring to the executions of collaborators by the Palestinian Authority, not to the liquidations by our forces..."

Professor S.: "Pardon me, pardon me. I thought you were asking me... In any case, about the Palestinians: it is disgusting, nauseating. This is how a dictatorial system operates. Absolutely unacceptable, shocking."

I am thinking about Samson and the Philistines. And about Khalil's attack on the road to Gaza – was it planned or unplanned? The news broadcast is still bothering me. Not so much for what it included as for what it did not. What are we being told each day? What are we being shown, and not shown? Who is missing? Names and faces...

In the month of January, sixteen Palestinians were killed by Israeli security forces: Sabri (50), Mahmud (37), Arij (22), Fatma (22), 'Abd al-Hamid al Kharti (38), Muhammad Abu Suf (27), 'Abd al-Hamid Khanfar (27), Ibrahim (70), Shaker (21), Mahdi (18), Muhammad Sharif (16), Khalil (22), Safwat (17), Muhammad Abu Musa (24), Isma'il (50), and Saber (38).

And then, in February, before Valentine's Day, how many more? Do we even know? The statistics are gleaned from a human rights organization, not from the Israeli press. I cannot remember having seen a photograph of a single one of these dead.

•

On the day following Valentine's Day, it is very early and very dark when I set off for the Ministry of Interior Office on Nablus Road – the infamous "Cage." This is not my idea of a good time, but there isn't much choice; a colleague at the college where I teach has been having ID trouble. Daoud's story is not unusual: Palestinian, mid-twenties, married with two small kids. His wife was born in Jerusalem and so has a blue-colored Jerusalem resident card issued by Israel. Daoud, however, was born in Bethlehem; his ID card is orange, and was issued by the Israeli Army through an office euphemistically called the Civil Administration.

Daoud cannot legally be in Jerusalem – even though his wife and her entire family have lived here for generations – without a special military transit permit. He had one, but it expired. So he asked a lawyer to write a letter to the Ministry of Interior asking for a blue ID card so that he can continue to live with his wife and children inside Jerusalem without breaking the law.

Forms needed to be filled out. A two-year trial period would have to be successfully navigated. At first, there is hope that Daoud will eventually get his Jerusalem ID and all will be well.

Not so fast. Israel held elections, the government changed, Daoud's request was denied, and, overnight, he became a virtual fugitive. Now he is stopped repeatedly on the street by IDF soldiers conducting random checks. "Get your papers sorted out or we'll end up arresting you," they tell him. "You'll be fined, or even jailed."

Should Daoud move his family to Bethlehem? His wife will have to forfeit her blue card, they will both be banished from Jerusalem forever. Should he keep under cover, and continue to come to work, risking punishment? Even if he never crosses a checkpoint along the "Green Line," he is in constant danger of random police searches on every street. His incriminating orange card will eventually get him in trouble.

Daoud and I have discussed it. Since for him to be in the streets is risky, I will take his file to the Ministry and find out what he needs to move things along. Has Daoud's lawyer tried this? "Oh," he says, "my lawyer wrote a couple of letters." Did the lawyer go over to the Cage to ask about it? "Oh, no," says Daoud, "my lawyer would never do that. You know what it is like over there!"

I do indeed. But never mind. The morning after Valentine's Day, I am wearing my invisibility cloak and my super protective "Not Looking a Bit Like a Palestinian Today" demeanor. I walk over to the Ministry, a sheaf of Daoud's letters and request forms in hand.

It is 5 a.m., cold and wet. Around twenty men are already waiting close to the entrance to the Ministry building, huddled under a six-by-two-foot tattered sheet of red and white plastic. We are near the barbershop with its *Golden Saloon* sign. A much smaller sign wired to the Cage says: *Ministry of Interior – Population Administration*. I walk up and stand in line. It is beginning to rain.

For the next three hours, I hear from the "population" about "administration." A man in a windbreaker with a *Denim Adventure* label has a story like Daoud's: he is there for a blue ID so he can live with his family in Jerusalem. His wife eventually appears, the baby bundled in a pink blanket. They stand in the rain, waiting. Another man in a *USA* ski cap is there for a Jordanian friend who has a Jerusalem wife. I hear the same complaint, over and over: "We just want to live with our families, to work, to survive. The Israelis want us not to exist."

At 6 a.m., a hawker comes by with tiny glasses of very thick Arabic coffee for two shekels. Before I know it, *Denim Adventure* has pressed a glass into my hand, ignoring my protests. People keep joining the crowded line, confined by two iron railings. Suddenly there is a flurry of activity up there by the still-locked turnstile leading into the Cage. Angry gesticulations, raised voices, negotiating. What's going on?

A young guy perched on one of the railings tells me this is normal:

"It's just the guy who got here at midnight, selling his place in line."

"Selling his place?"

"*Aiywah!* He comes in the middle of the night and stands by the entrance. When the line gets long enough he sells his place for 100 shekels to some desperate guy who can't afford to not get in. Maybe a sick child, or a friend in prison, you know – something that can't wait a month or two."

So the early bird sells his desperate brother a better chance to get some justice, and arrives home for breakfast with a day's salary already in his pocket. Occupation creates entrepreneurs.

At 7 a.m., a very scruffy fellow arrives in a threadbare English tweed jacket and filthy gray plastic flip-flops, pulls a portable manual Hebrew language typewriter from a shopping bag, squats down on the sidewalk, and sets up his office on an overturned cardboard box. This is the scribe, who will translate the needed information and type out forms in readable Hebrew for 10 shekels a page. Soon, a line forms for his services. Inevitably, some folks try to haggle the price down.

At least 100 people are here now. New additions climb over the railings and join their friends-and-relations in line (to the tune of "*Hopah*! Where's your 100 shekels? *Esh Maalak?* Where do you think you are going?!"). The mass gets denser and denser. We are now packed in so tightly that I cannot move my arms. I can feel 360 degrees of men's bodies against mine, I keep my breath shallow and hope for the best.

I turn to *Denim Adventure*. "Too bad my wife didn't come along!"

He grins, nodding. "Is real *picnic*!" he says.

I can't help asking, "So…why are we crammed together like this? Why doesn't everyone just back up a bit – there's plenty of room on the sidewalk! We would all breath a little easier!"

He shrugs. "We are men of street," he says. "Upstairs, are ten rooms empty. Israel want us like this…waiting, standing, crowd, wet."

Under my left shoulder, a short man is carefully scrutinizing the Hebrew article on the front page of *Yediot Ahronot*. Images of the attack on the Gaza Road, the mutilated *Egged* bus on the sidewalk, the faces of the victims, fill the page. Below, a distant shot shows the end of the chase, police roughly dragging Khalil from the driver's seat. Someone at my other elbow mutters in Arabic. "*Miskineh!*" "Poor guy!" – is that what he said? I can't be sure.

You can't see Khalil's face. A trusted driver. A simple man. A ruthless killer. The Israeli columnist writes: "Today's bus driver can easily become tomorrow's terrorist."

Easily. Just like that.

Egged is a good name for a bus company. In Hebrew the word means "connection." To "take a bus" is to "get the connection." Israel's citizens spend a long time at bus stops. My son Jonathan was only ten when he told me the old Israeli bus stop joke.

A woman is waiting at a bus stop in Tel Aviv. She thinks: should I wait for the bus or take a taxi? If I take a taxi, all well and good. But if I wait for the bus, it will be crowded. If there is standing room only, all well and good. But if I find a seat, one of two things. Either I sit next to a woman or I sit next to a man. If I sit next to a woman, all well and good. But if I sit next to a man, either he will be handsome or ugly. If he is ugly, all well and good. But if he is handsome, either we will fall in love or not. If we don't fall in love, all well and good. But if we do fall in love, either he will ask me to marry him or he will emigrate to the USA. If he emigrates, all well and good. But if we get married, either we will have children or not. If we don't have children, all well and good. But if we do have children, either they will be handicapped or healthy. If they are all handicapped, all well and good. But if they are all healthy, either they will be drafted into the IDF or they will get out on a psychological profile. If they get out on a psychological profile, all well and good. But if they are drafted, they will either get desk jobs or join combat units. If they get desk jobs, all well and good. But if they join combat units, either they will stay out of the Occupied Territories, or they will be stationed at a checkpoint somewhere. If they stay out of the Territories, all well and good. But if they get posted to some horrible checkpoint in Gaza...! You know what, I think I'll take a taxi!

Get the connection?

At the Cage, it is 8 a.m. The turnstile is opened by the soldiers and a stampede begins up the narrow stairs. If it were not for *Denim Adventure* and his strong shoulder, I might not have made it through the turnstile in one piece, so heavy was the crush.

Upstairs, over two hundred men, women and children wait their turn to be "administered." They clutch their tattered ID cards or other papers cranked out of the old sidewalk *Olympia*. A woman in a worn embroidered dress goes up to an armed guard, showing him her paper, some kind of summons. The Israeli guard is young, long hair in a neat ponytail and a ring in his ear, packing two guns, one on each side. He takes a look.

"What do you want from me?" he asks. "It says here you should show up at 8 a.m. It's already half past. You'd better go try in the next room."

The woman hesitates, her face blank and drawn, then crumples the paper into her fist and moves away. The guard exchanges a glance with a pretty female clerk behind the desk, they both snigger.

It all takes a very long time. I get out of the Cage before noon, with very little to report. A polite clerk has managed to extract from some file a fuzzy old letter from the Ministry, addressed to Daoud's wife. This letter (which I am sure was never sent) asks her to clarify details of the family's municipal tax bill from last year and a couple of other items. Maybe, just maybe, if these details are provided, the Ministry will look at the file again. Maybe, just maybe, Daoud will not be so likely to be harassed by soldiers on his way to work. Maybe.

Daoud is absurdly delighted. "You got in! You got a letter! Thank you so much! My lawyer will know what to do with this! When can you go back?"

Since 1967, when Israel occupied ("united") Arab East Jerusalem, the Arab population of the city has grown to around 200,000. Of these, over 15,000 have had their Jerusalem ID cards removed against their wishes, and they face legal problems if they remain in Jerusalem. Many more await processing of their ID status.

However, attempts to discourage Palestinians from staying in their native city are not working. Today one out of every three Jerusalem residents is an Arab, and holds a blue Jerusalem ID, apparently identical to those of Jewish citizens. But these Arabs are not citizens. Inside the ID card, in the space marked *Nationality*, there is just a blank. These folks are "non-citizen residents" in their own city. Unable to vote in the national elections, they cannot determine Israel's policy toward them. Simply put, it is a policy of segregation and harassment – defined by one Israeli analyst as "Don't swallow them, but don't spit them out."

Arabs comprise 30% of the city's population, but Arab East Jerusalem receives 5% of municipal funding. In Jewish neighborhoods of the city, the government has built 40,000 apartments, not a single one in Arab Jerusalem. In one year, $10 million was garnered in city taxes from Arab residents. Only $2 million of that was reinvested in East Jerusalem.

And so forth. Get the connection?

An experienced dialogue expert, Arnold Mindell, writes:

> The basic goals of…marginalized people who resort to violence are…economic support, freedom and the respect necessary to survive. Calling them 'terrorists' is useless… Remember that those who have been hurt have always had to enlighten the mainstream… Until

someone understands the terrorist.

"Understand the terrorist?" No. We condemn terrorists, who are always villains from outside our camp. We mourn the dead, but only if they are "ours." Meanwhile, the Occupation has created the perfect machine to turn bus drivers into killers. Hundreds of thousands of Palestinians desire only bread, freedom and respect, but we keep them faceless and hopeless until they snap. We keep them caged and frustrated until they bite, and then we wonder why they kill people at random, "just like that." An awful lot goes into making a terrorist; it is not "easy" or "inevitable." Daily humiliation is a factory for killers, especially when we close our ears and minds, and – yes – our hearts, to the inaudible scream of the dispossessed.

FROM A DISTANCE
Jerusalem, 6th March 2001

Last night, and also the night before that, the guns sounded and the sirens wailed. We heard them from our bedroom in East Jerusalem in the early hours. I got up again and again, moving from window to window. Those shots, were they from the Ramallah Road, or Psagot? Maybe from Beit Jala or the Tunnel Road? At a distance, it was hard to tell. The sirens rose and fell, receded. Nearby, a car alarm was blasting the night, but surely that was just because a sudden east wind was shaking the nearby trees. I closed the windows, one by one (to keep the cold out, I thought to myself) and went back to bed.

On February 22nd, at 3:15 in the morning, Roni Natanel (33) was driving his Fiat Uno through the French Hill Junction where the Ramallah Road enters Jerusalem. Four Palestinians stopped him and asked, "Which way to the Old City?" He told them they were going the wrong way. One of them pulled out a Kalashnikov and sprayed him with bullets. It was not that he was impertinent; it was just that his accent identified him as Jewish. Leaving Roni bleeding, the attackers roared off in their Mitsubishi and disappeared into the distance. This is the fourth shooting at the French Hill Junction in two months. We are not going much to the French Hill supermarket these days – certainly not at 3:15 in the morning.

February 23rd was a Friday. Ra'id Musa (21) was shot and killed – "from a distance" says the newspaper – near the Tunnel Road linking Jerusalem with the Israeli settlements to the south. The Tunnel Road is a multi-million dollar bypass-*cum*-death-trap hovering between Gilo and Beit Jala. I wonder if Ra'id was tending his sheep near the Tunnel Road, or trying to get home from prayers in the El Aqsa Mosque, or – conversely – sneaking up on Gilo with an incendiary device, or trying to plant a bomb under one of the bridges. "From a distance" can mean a lot of different things. "From a distance" can mean an accident – or it can mean a professional sniping.

Israeli snipers are outstanding. In *Haaretz* on November 20th, an Israeli sniper (oops – "sharpshooter") was interviewed; he really had quite a lot to say about his craft.

"A sharpshooter is like a pilot," he said. "His work is very clean, certain. A sharpshooter, from 200 meters, has no problem hitting the head. At 500 meters you already know not to aim at the head but the middle of the body, because it's easier. But at 100 meters it's almost sterile firing, very easy."

"Sterile firing?"

Of course there are Palestinian snipers too. Otherwise, the windows in the Jewish neighborhood of Gilo would not be so heavily sandbagged. "Usually the Palestinian fire is pathetic," says the Israeli sharpshooter. "The shooting is totally pathetic…you know that most of it will be in the air. Even if it's pathetic, you have to return fire."

You just have to. And, of course, you should know the age of those you are shooting at. After all, the IDF has rules of engagement.

> Israeli Sniper: "You don't shoot at a child of 12 or under."
> Interviewer: "So a child of 12 or older is allowed?"
> Sniper: "12 and up is allowed. He's not a child anymore. He's already after his bar mitzvah. Something like that."
> Interviewer: "Under International Law, a child is defined as someone up to the age of 18."
> Sniper: "Up until 18 is a child?"
> Interviewer: "So according to the IDF, it is 12?"
> Sniper: "According to what the I.D.F. says to its soldiers.
> I don't know what it says to the media."

That settles it then.

On February 3rd, a soldier of the Givati Brigade fired a 22 gauge sniper rifle at 'Issa Ibrahim al-Amur (14). He was hit in the stomach and died later of his wounds. I guess this means that the shot was fired from a distance of 500 meters – otherwise, why not just hit him in the head and be done with it?

'Issa – at 500 meters – must have posed a serious threat to the Givati Brigade soldier. Let's see. If 'Issa had a bomb strapped to his 14-year-old body, or a Kalashnikov under his arm, or maybe a very powerful slingshot in the pocket of his pants... From a distance, it's hard to be sure. But not hard to make a perfect hit with a 22 gauge sniper rifle.

The soldier who shot him was never indicted for his killing of 14-year-old 'Issa. Instead, in a field court presided over by his commanding officer, he was found to have violated "norms and orders in the sector" (the words of the IDF spokesman). The unnamed army sharpshooter received a jail sentence for killing 'Issa; the sentence is 49 days. A good portion of the sentence may be served at a considerable distance from the prison.

Almost 400 Palestinians have been killed since October in this conflict. Not a single Israeli soldier has been indicted before a military court, to say nothing of a civil court.

Keep it at a distance, right?

An Israeli analyst recently wrote an article titled *"In defense of a fence."* This is about a proposed Israeli policy called "Unilateral Separation" – a euphemism for building an electronically wired wall around some parts of the West Bank and Gaza and keeping over 3 million Palestinians there until they starve – or go away. Quite a few otherwise "sensible" Israelis (and some non-Israelis too) think this is a dandy idea. After all, writes this analyst, "the American proverb that 'good fences make good neighbors' is relevant to the Israeli-Palestinian conflict too."

Poor Robert Frost must be rolling over in his grave. Doesn't anyone remember that his often-badly-quoted poem *Mending Wall* is actually a *condemnation* – not in praise – of separation?

With a primitive and fearful mindset, Frost's farmer neighbor wants to contain every communicating passion with a tidy wall of rock; he needs to repair stone walls even where they are irrelevant.

> *Something there is that doesn't love a wall...*

— that is the way the poem starts. That "something" is natural freedom, pure and simple. The poet sees the unruly groundswell of it, arching with disturbing beauty between him and his mole-blind and security-minded neighbor, who is trapped in the shadowy caution of his ancestors, needing to be enlightened, not emulated. "I see him there," writes Frost, "like an old-stone savage armed." But no walls, however "traditional," can keep the impetus to freedom underground for long.

•

Far to the north, in pastoral Galilee, among the scrub-oak forests and the almond and olive groves, a small group of us stand around Father Kamal, looking out over the overgrown piles of rubble that is the destroyed village of Bir'am. The priest's voice is soft, but very clear. "This is my village. That is our house, over there, where the almond tree is growing out of the wall. Over there is the ancient synagogue. My parents always told us: 'Don't play in the synagogue, respect it.'"

We peer into the emptiness of tottering old walls, brambles, doorways. The homes are roofless and shapeless. On the lintels, the ancient crosses have been effaced by vandals zealous to push the past away. Today this is a National Park. Israeli guides show tourists the synagogue and talk about the Jewish community in the Byzantine period. "The Arabs," they say, "left in 1948." The brochure says: "During the War of Independence, the villagers were evacuated."

Kamal smiles. "When I come here now I have to pay an entrance fee," he says. "Over there is the new Jewish community built on the farmland of Bir'am. The immigrants who live there use our land, we cannot go there. Here in the village is our Maronite church, all locked up. We are allowed here for weddings and funerals. Years ago I came here and found that the *kibbutzniks* were keeping cows in the church. So I went to the court and got permission to lock up the church, but to use it for our days of feasting and mourning. In the summer we have the youth camp here. That is all."

Kamal looks out over the surrounding hills. "I remember that day in 1948. I was just 4 years old. I was among the children who lined the road leading into the village, holding bowls of bread and salt, symbols of hospitality, for the Jewish soldiers coming into the village. A week later, they told us we would have to leave for a while, to open a way for the army to move through, going north. We could come back in 15 days, they said. We believed them. Until today, those 15 days have not ended."

"We camped in the valley for three weeks, waiting. It was winter, and cold. We moved north, passing into Lebanon. And then Spring came. Israel's President promised that the rights of the Maronite Christians would be respected, so we returned. We came back to live with our relatives in Gish, right over there on the hill. I remember when we came back, my family was walking, and I was riding on a goat. We came a long way. We were hoping that soon we could go back to our houses in Bir'am. But the Army said no, so, stranded in Gish, we waited."

"On November 11th in 1953, the Israeli Air Force came. We watched from that hillside, right there. We still call it the Wailing Hill. The planes dropped their bombs on Bir'am, each bomb destroying a roof, a home. You can see, here below us, the walls are still standing, because the roofs were so neatly destroyed, from above. We watched, and we cried and cried."

As for us, we stand, like the walls, embarrassed and silent. What should we do with the memories of this Galilean priest? Can the ghosts of the past walk home into the chaos of the present?

What can we ever understand about the real distance between the Galilee of sixty years ago and the Gaza of today?

Far to the south, on another planet, the Israeli settlement of Har Homa is today being bulldozed into the expropriated West Bank Palestinian lands of Beit Sahour. A Jewish contractor, supervising the construction at Har Homa, employing hundreds of Palestinian workers on the building site, sums up the whole story with a lugubrious sigh:

> These Palestinians are getting too big for their britches. They even speak to you as one equal to another. The Palestinian wants bread, and then he wants butter, and then he wants *your* bread. Don't trust these Palestinians.

The dictates of fear are finding their voices:

> Give them an inch and they'll take a mile! First they want Gaza and Ramallah, then they want Bir'am! Finally, they will want Tel Aviv! Stop these Arab fantasies of 'return' before they go too far! What's a terrorist? A gun-toting refugee who wants to come home. So let's build a wall! Unilateral Separation! National Security!

The voices, insidious or strident, mingle in a violent wind around us and within us. At night, when the shooting begins, it is especially hard to tell which direction the sounds are coming from, and what they require of our sleeping hearts. Freedom or vengeance? Security or brutality? We try not to listen. And – for as long as we are able – we keep our distance.

LETTER TO A PALESTINIAN CHRISTIAN
Jerusalem, 12th April 2001

Dear N.,

For six months, as the violence has been raging around us, I have been sending out my reflections on "the situation," my cries of pain, my musings of hope. My essays have expressed shock, frustration and anger at Israeli policies. It is my conviction (which I have made very clear) that the continuing Occupation of the Palestinian homeland by Israel is the pivotal pragmatic issue in this struggle. The Occupation inhibits peace, threatens Israel's security and integrity, and must come to an end. The chief responsibility for this lies with Israel.

However, there is more. The Palestinian people, as disadvantaged and abused as they are, also have a responsibility for their own destiny. Here I have been much more hesitant in speaking out. How can someone from "outside," however supportive, say to a humiliated nation: "You too have sinned!" Still, what must be said must be said.

Thank you, N., for being able to listen. You do not claim to be "representative" of all or even most Palestinians – no one could claim that! But as an Arab Christian clergyman you have spoken out for justice in Palestine while at the same time refusing to demonize Israel. You, a refugee and a victim of hatred, still refuse to hate. Perhaps, then, you can translate my thoughts into words that others will not find hateful. Perhaps your fellow Palestinians will hear these words, not as condemnation but as the strongest form of encouragement.

Today is the time for Palestinians and Israelis – who together recognize the systemic evil of this Occupation – to turn wholeheartedly to the nonviolent way. The way to Palestinian independence – *and* Israel's security – has reached a crossroad; from this point, those who care about the moral future of their emerging nation can only walk one path.

Palestinians need to consider. The time of the "liberation buffet" is past. To mix declarations of moral right with blood-curdling suicide missions against civilian targets, with snipings, lynchings and fire-bombings, is not admissible. Glorifying the famous "David's slingshot," the rock- and bottle-hurling "freedom kids," is no longer right, if it ever was.

It is time to envision the end, not exalt the means. Gandhi taught that a violent struggle yields only a violent freedom. Can you, a leader of your people, say that a violent freedom is better than no freedom at all? Or is such desperation a recipe for social and spiritual death? If one limb is sick, the whole body is ill. If one heart is filled with hatred, all suffer. Every life is precious, the weak and the strong alike. As hard as it is to say this under the shadow of the systemic brutality of the Occupation, still it must be said. Two wrongs never made a right; killing the oppressor does not give the oppressed the higher moral ground.

But what other option do the oppressed have? In the first weeks of this *Intifada*, a Palestinian analyst wrote that the use of firearms against the Israeli Army was futile. His opinion was purely pragmatic, not "tainted" with moral overtones; still, it was ignored. More recently, Bassam Eid and Edward Said have advocated a nonviolent resistance movement. You yourself have called on the hearts of your Christian Arab community to decry, with a single voice, violence on both sides.

Regardless of all this, armed resistance is still seen as the "first choice." The killing goes on. Over 400 Palestinians have died in the past six months, and thousands are wounded. A score of Israelis have been killed; still, Israel is seen by many – both here and abroad – as the victim. How is this possible? A recent brilliant study in London's *The Guardian* shows how media bias prompts journalists to suppress brutal truths about Israel's policies. But does this totally explain why Palestinians are still seen as violent troublemakers?

Palestine is losing the image war. Although Israel's policies of Occupation are as wrong as racial segregation in the US and apartheid in South Africa, still Israel's image is that of a reasonable nation daily barraged by thousands of hateful Palestinian attacks.

You have made justice your goal, and I have been honored to pray with you, to march with you. Together we stood at the gates of the Old City holding our placards: "*God Requires Justice!*" Together we walked to the Israeli Army roadblock, singing "*We Shall Overcome!*" We visited the bombed homes of the bereaved from Ramallah to Beit Jala. It is easy for us to say: "We have done all we can." It is harder to admit: "We can do better."

As a pastor, you preach words of hope to your people in this virtual slavery of closure and siege. You teach that freedom does not mean revenge or "getting even." You teach that we begin our Exodus with an examination of our hearts. You say:

> To lift the Occupation does not mean the destruction of Israel. On the contrary, it means a new life and security for Israel. To lift the Occupation is to end the injustice, the violence, the humiliation, and everything that oppresses and dehumanizes. Indeed, to end the Occupation is the beginning of the humanization of Israel. We must work with God to end the Occupation. We must free Palestine.

Still the Occupation continues, and conditions are worse today than they were six months ago. Violence and counter-violence spin out of control.

One Sunday, the Jewish community of Hebron buried a 10-month-old baby, Shalhevet, shot in the head by Palestinian fire. The next day, Palestinians buried 11-year-old Mahmud, killed by heavy Israeli machine gun fire in his home near Hebron. The death of these innocents has not halted the grief, fury and slaughter; we seem no closer to freedom and humanity than before. Is there a path we have not yet tried?

Here is a story from another place and another time that may still bring us some guidance. In 1962, Martin Luther King was at a vulnerable point in his work. His sermons had failed to abolish segregation. He had been excommunicated from the National Baptist Convention. The centennial of Lincoln's Emancipation Proclamation had come and gone with no presidential commitment to de-segregation. To make matters worse, the police killing of Ronald Stokes and shooting of seven other black men outside a Muslim shrine in Los Angeles a year earlier had strengthened the call for black revenge. King's nonviolent sit-ins and Freedom Rides were the object of ridicule for the Nation of Islam. Malcolm X sneered: "An old woman can sit. A coward can sit. It takes a man to stand." The word on the street was "fight." The black community seemed anything but ready for a committed nonviolent campaign for civil rights.

It must have been tempting for King to admit defeat, or to close himself into a defensive desperation. What happened instead might make us pause. We need not act alone; our ally in justice may appear from an unexpected quarter, so we need to keep our eyes open, and our hearts too.

In January 1963, at the National Conference on Religion and Race held in Chicago, Dr. King shared the podium with a remarkable man – the Jewish theologian Rabbi Abraham Heschel. The combination was electrifying. The Baptist preacher from Atlanta and the Hasidic visionary from Warsaw spoke, incredibly, the same language. They both quoted Amos: "Let justice roll down like waters, and righteousness like a mighty stream." They both called for a modern prophetic witness in the struggle for justice – a "voice that God has lent to the silent agony" of the oppressed.

We do not know how much the insights of the old rabbi strengthened King's resolve in the path he had already chosen.

What we do know is his next step: the focused genius of the Birmingham campaign, where black and white, northerner and southerner, Muslim and Christian and Jew and atheist, all marched and were arrested together in the greatest nonviolent initiative since Gandhi's March to the Sea.

The rest is history; not a distant or alien history but one that affects us directly here and now. You, too, N., sometimes feel misunderstood, ineffective. You, too, sometimes feel nourished by the prophetic voices of your Jewish neighbors, for whom the justice of Amos is a higher calling than any tribal holiness Leviticus can offer. You, too, in your commitment to nonviolence, share King's realization (in Taylor Branch's words) that "unmerited suffering was required to supplement reason in a selfish world...for breaking through to guarded or disinterested strangers."

What would it mean to choose the path of "unmerited suffering" – *willingly*? What would it mean, here and today, to send to the "enemy" messages of nonviolent resolve rather than the stones and bullets of desperation? What would it mean to enlist the aid of non-Palestinians, to honor their value and even their advice, in a struggle that is not a tribal "holy war" but a bid for universal justice? I do not know the answers, but I know the questions must be asked. Can you, N., as a pastor and a leader in Palestine, ask these questions? Can you be the voice that not only comforts but challenges too?

Ask this: Is it freedom that you seek, or are you content with punishing your enemies? If freedom is your goal, can you choose the more effective risk, not the more satisfying, the most moral means, not the most popular? Which will it be?

Ask this: Do you agree with Gaza's Dr. El-Sarraj: "Liberation of...Palestinians from the Israeli Occupation...from the humiliation and suffering, will happen when Israelis are liberated from their fear and insecurity. Palestinian bullets only strengthen

Israelis' sense of victimization and paranoia." If you agree, what will you do about it?

Ask this: Do you see the human face in the soldier at the checkpoint? Is it possible that his aggression might be encouraged – at least in part – by our own bitterness and anger? What can be done about that?

Ask this: Is it more courageous to blow up a bus, to aim a rifle at a settlement, to shoot a soldier on duty, to knife a shopper in the market, or to confront an Israeli tank and hurl a stone? Are these equally courageous? Are these the only forms of courage available? Would you point to a stone-throwing crowd and call it a "nonviolent demonstration?" Is this the best we can do?

Ask this: Does anyone understand that the lone and *unarmed* Chinese student facing a government tank will be a more enduring witness to human liberation than all of the stones thrown in Palestine? That the woman who stands *unarmed* in front of the army bulldozer as it advances to destroy Palestinian olive trees is a more enduring witness than the suicide bomber who destroys Jew and Arab together in a random attack?

Then ask this: Are we ready for the kind of struggle that will defeat evil with love, that will break hearts of stone, and not just the iron bars of closure? Are we ready to put aside prejudice, to join hands with the Israeli activists who have a common cause with us against the Occupation, and against violence – *all violence?*

You have the means and the voice to ask these questions. If the answers are courageous, then the way forward is marked by the example of those who were at this crossroad before us. They chose nonviolent action rather than revenge; theirs was the voice of prophets; their path the way to freedom. We certainly will not walk that way alone.

Salamat and Shalom,
Henry R. Carse

A HOME IN ANATA
Jerusalem, 6th May 2001

On Friday the 13th of April, which happened to be Good Friday, I made a little pilgrimage to Anata. Just in case you were wondering, Anata is biblical Anathoth, hometown of Jeremiah the prophet. You are thinking that I had a fairly biblical Good Friday, but it wasn't quite that simple.

I don't suppose there was ever an inscription anywhere in Anata marking some house or other as "Jeremiah's birthplace." If there were, it would probably not have survived the recent Israeli Army house-crushings in old Jerry's neighborhood. Twenty-eight Palestinian homes were destroyed by Israel's intrepid Defense Forces in demolitions operations throughout the Palestinian Territories in the week between April 6th and 13th. This is just the beginning; Israel's civil authorities, emulating the military, now intend to destroy another nineteen Arab homes in East Jerusalem as well.

Since October 2000, over 500 homes have been demolished by Israeli tank fire and bulldozers. This is just the tip of the iceberg; since the Occupation began in 1967, a total of 7,000 Palestinian residences have been leveled, mostly by orders wielded (if that is the right word) by the military authorities (oddly called the "Civil Administration") in the Occupied Territories. All this house-bashing has left 40,000 Palestinians homeless.

Demolition orders are issued for structures without building permits. You are thinking this is reasonable; everyone should get municipal permits before building. Palestinians apply for permits. Even in East Jerusalem, which is in principal not ruled by the army, such permits are nearly impossible to get. Let us forget for a moment that Arab residents of East Jerusalem are required to pay municipal taxes although they are not citizens of the state, and that they live in very crowded conditions as compared to the Jewish neighborhoods of West Jerusalem. Let's not mention the fact that one third of East Jerusalem has been confiscated from Palestinians and zoned for Jewish development only, and more than half of the rest of East Jerusalem has been frozen as "green areas." Let's just say that any of the 200,000 Arab residents of East Jerusalem who applies for a building permit is not too surprised when the request is denied.

Remarkably enough, however, 80% of all building violations are in the Jewish neighborhoods of West Jerusalem and only 20% in the Arab neighborhoods of East Jerusalem. Is it just an unfortunate coincidence that 80% of the houses demolished by municipal order belong to Arabs, and only 20% are Jewish homes? Or is it simply that the Arab homes just aren't quite the same?

Arab families – desperate for a roof over their heads – often live in houses with no permits. Take the Shawamreh family in East Jerusalem, for example. Salim and his wife Arabiyeh applied – *four times* – for a building permit for their existing home. First, the permit was denied because their house is on land zoned as "agricultural." Jewish contractors can get zoning rulings changed, Arabs cannot. However, as luck would have it, the Israel Land Authorities decided to change the zoning themselves, since they wanted to use the land for development. So... Salim applied again, and was denied, this time because the slope was too steep. He adjusted the plans and applied again. Denied: the Land Authorities have a gigantic bypass road planned. He applied again, and this time he was told that he needed the signatures of two Anata residents who had rights in the property. Salim had no idea who these two people might be, and the Land Authorities would not tell him. So, with a crew of human rights activists helping out, Salim and Arabiyeh went around and got the signatures of every single resident of Anata. They filed once again for the building permit. Instead, before they could say "Oslo!" – they got a demolition order.

Salim and Arabiyeh, with their children Amir, Muhammad, Wafa'a, Ashraf and Lena, hosted us in Anata on Good Friday. We had warmish soft drinks under a tattered almond tree with a single plastic chair under it, surrounded by dust and cement chunks. This is what remains of the Shawamreh house, bulldozed into oblivion. We had come to Anata to clear the foundation in order to build again.

The Shawamreh home was first demolished in July 1998, leveled by bulldozer and pneumatic drill right down to the foundation. Arabiyeh inhaled tear gas and Salim was badly beaten as they tried to prevent the soldiers from destroying their home. In the disturbance that ensued, a neighbor kid was shot and lost his kidney, and Salim and Arabiyeh's 4-year-old son was so traumatized that he ran away and spent the night hiding behind a rock, only turning up the next day.

Immediately, the Israeli Coalition Against House Demolitions, working with Rabbis for Human Rights and other Israeli activist groups, rebuilt the Shawamreh home. Demolitions crews of the "Civil Administration" showed up in early August and demolished the house again. The Palestinian Land Defense Committee, with the help of Israeli organizations, rebuilt the house a third time.

By this time, Israel's government had changed, Barak was in office, and the house was allowed to stand for eight whole months – just long enough for the Shawamreh family to begin to feel at home. Then, Sharon took power, and the mechanisms of Israel's "Matrix of Control" in the Occupied Territories went into high gear. A few days before Good Friday, the army once more razed the house down to the foundation. Not a trace remains but huge piles of cracked stone and pulverized cement.

The entire process is documented in photographs. Here you see Rami and Micha, the cheerful guys in charge of the IDF demolition crew. They stand in the doorway of the home, dressed in casual civvies, surrounded by soldiers in olive drab. Rami has his Galil rifle slung low and at the ready, with his finger on the trigger guard. He and his sidekick Micha are the cruelest looking thugs I have ever seen, but then, I haven't checked out mug shots of Milosevic's goons. Rami and Micha destroy homes. Knitted brows, eyes slid over sideways, stubble on their chins; I can't tell whether they could be said to enjoy their work, but they certainly take it seriously. Rami's cousins own the bulldozer company that gets the contracts from the army for this kind of dirty work. It's a neat little in-house arrangement – no pun intended.

Here are photos of the demolition in progress. First, the doomed home has to be emptied of its contents; for this, the contractors use foreign workers. Here they are, lanky laborers from Ghana, hopefully not totally oblivious to irony as they toss Palestinian furniture and toys and kitchenware out the windows and drag clothes and blankets into a big pile under the almond tree.

Then the bulldozer moves in, a D9 big enough to make short work of a cinder-block structure. The photos are a bit out of focus here. Dust, big slabs of cement at odd angles, family members crying. For the foundation, a gigantic pneumatic drill is more efficient than a blade, so at that point the dozer wields a drill like a giant arm and pulverizes what remains.

The dust settles, Rami and Micha pack up their soldiers and Ghanans and Galil rifles and D9's and roar off at the head of the convoy in their IDF jeeps. It is all over until next time. And there will be a next time.

It is Good Friday. We stand on the pile of rubble, shocked and disgusted, ready to rebuild. But we are also aware of the enormity of the whole thing. Not only is the house doomed, again and again; the entire area is slated for take-over. To the southeast we can see the red-tile rooftops of Ma'ale Adumim, a veteran Israeli settlement of the Jerusalem-Jericho "corridor" – a broad slash through the Occupied Territories and a key axis of Israeli control. Ma'ale Adumim is over 5 kilometers distant from Anata, but the intervening hills and valleys, farmlands and pasturelands, situated over the richest underground water resource in

Palestine, were all "annexed" by Israel in the 90s for Jewish settlement development.

Now, Sharon's government is making the "annexation" of this corridor permanent, thus controlling the Palestinian aquifer and (incidentally) reducing Palestinian autonomous land areas in the West Bank by 48%. The *de facto* size of Ma'ale Adumim now exceeds that of Tel Aviv. It is the largest settlement block in the Occupied Territories – maybe in the world. Israel now can go ahead and build tens of thousands of residential units (for Jews only, of course) on Palestinian land, and all without straying from the letter of the Oslo Accords. No "new settlement" is being introduced; it's just good old Ma'ale Adumim, doing a little "natural growth." And, as incredible as it seems, Anata is simply in the way.

Starkly put, from the ruins of the Shawamreh home we are gazing upon the ruins of the Two State Solution. Territorial integrity for a future Palestinian nation is neatly decapitated by the Ma'ale Adumim corridor. Israel's "Matrix of Control" is absolute, and in those terms the Shawamreh home is simply an inconvenience. It poses an annoying question mark on the northern edge of a massive Jewish settlement area. If the Shawamrehs remain, how can the IDF construct the bypass roads, the military camps and the security fences and other necessities of life every Israeli colony needs?

Salim and Arabiyeh and their children are not terrorists, criminals or revolutionaries, but they are certainly a nuisance to the Israeli Occupation. Their home just refuses to disappear into the dust, as the Occupation's architects wish. And here we are, ex-pats and Israeli activists and internationals, in denims and T-shirts, a handful of nuisances and nobodies, standing with the Shawamrehs so that they will not rebuild alone. Under the April sun, we handle the rough concrete and the dusty stones that will one day shelter the Shawamreh family, even if only for as long as it takes for a D9 to come up the slope.

We are observing Good Friday in the best way we can, by clearing rubble and shifting stone for a little resurrection.

Politicians and warlords cannot forever control the destiny of a people desiring to be free. The Israeli public cannot stay ignorant forever of the systemic evil that the Occupation brings daily into the lives of thousands. The world, so preoccupied with Space Tourists and Spice Girls, cannot ignore forever the cry of the poor whose homes are crushed by the violence of the righteous rich. The goons and moguls of the "Matrix of Control" will some day be called to account.

It's old Jerry the prophet who says so:

> Behold I will restore the fortunes of the tents
> of Jacob, and have compassion on his dwellings...
> Out of them will come songs of thanksgiving,
> and the voices of rejoicing... As I have watched
> over them to pluck up and break down, to over-
> throw, destroy and bring evil, so I will watch
> over them to build and to plant, says the Lord.

That was a long time ago. Anata was a village occupied by the army of Babylon, poised to destroy Jerusalem. Jeremiah himself became an exile; he saw despair like this, and destruction too. He was a prophet, so he knew how to be a nuisance. He accused the powerful, and suffered for it. Compassionate of heart, he cried his share of tears, but he was tough too, and ready to rebuild. He never accepted that despair would endure. He saw beyond the Ramis and the Michas and the demolition orders and D9's of his day, and knew that hope would come, cradled in the arms of justice.

SOME PEOPLE MARCHING
Jerusalem, 16th April 2001

Holy Saturday dawned clear and cool. The ex-pats in town spent most of the day at the Church of the Holy Sepulcher for the Holy Fire Ceremony – the Orthodox Christian celebration of the resurrection. After this sacred pyrodrama, I set off with a couple of American friends who were wanting to spend the rest of the day with the fledgling Palestinian freedom movement. We had barely reached the bus station near Damascus Gate when a contingent of twelve volunteers from Norway caught up with us, eager to get to the freedom march in Bethlehem. By the time we reached the bus station, we were fifteen strong, so we just hired a mini-van and rode to the Bethlehem checkpoint in style.

The Norwegians were in earnest high spirits. They had been in town for only two days, after touring Syria and Jordan. On the ride to Bethlehem, they oohed and ahed over the fantastic view of King Herod's mountain tomb, and looked glum when told about the newest illegal Israeli settlement looming nearby on Har Homa. Every single one of these Norwegians came here to atone for the "Oslo Mistake." They intended to march and demonstrate to bring about a new peace process, this time one that "would not be a sell-out." A novel idea: Norwegian pangs of conscience over a flawed Oslo Peace Agreement that did not deliver justice in Israel and Palestine. It seemed to me that such scruples took Norwegian earnestness to a bit of an extreme.

Someone asked me, as we approached the checkpoint, to tell them a bit about the action awaiting us.

"Today's march is organized by Rapprochement Center in Beit Sahour," I informed them. "Rapprochement was founded in 1988, during the First *Intifada*, the first nonviolent action organization in modern Palestine. Today, the violence of the Second *Intifada* has ended most cooperation across the Israel/Palestine divide. So Rapprochement is working with something called the

Israeli *critical left*, a very small group of Israelis who have not given up on the peace movement and who still believe that the Occupation must end. Then, of course, there are international groups like yours, who support Palestinians' call for an end to the Israeli Occupation."

"The Palestinians are hoping to show that nonviolent action against the Occupation is possible even in the midst of the present violence. It is significant that they have picked a strongly fortified Israeli military checkpoint like the one between Jerusalem and Bethlehem. This checkpoint restricts Palestinian freedom of movement and freedom of worship. Christian Palestinians traditionally attend Holy Week services in Jerusalem, but those who are in Bethlehem are not allowed out for any reason. Closing off access to places of worship denies human rights protected in the Geneva Convention."

"Palestinian and international marchers intend to reach the checkpoint from the Bethlehem (Palestinian) side, and to pass through if possible, continuing up the road toward Jerusalem. A group of Israeli activists will be marching at the same time toward the checkpoint from the Israeli side. They plan to meet the Palestinians and 'intees' as they pass through the checkpoint, or at least give them moral support if there is a confrontation with the Israeli soldiers there."

"The message of the march is *Occupation is Violence! Stop the Violence!* It's a nonviolent challenge to Israeli Army conventions such as illegal closures and checkpoints. This march is a beginning of what will hopefully be a renewed popular nonviolent campaign to end the Occupation."

I was not sure how many of my Norwegian audience understood what I was saying; spontaneous translation was still going on when we reached the checkpoint itself. We drove up to the barricades, and my heart sank when I saw the beefed-up IDF presence, with several armored jeeps and a troop carrier. The soldier in our lane stopped the mini-van and questioned both the driver and myself, and finally let us into Bethlehem as "tourists on our way to pray" – a plausible tale if you have a flexible prayer life. I felt I should remind my companions that while it was fairly simple to pass through an Israeli checkpoint with foreign passports, this is not the case for Palestinians, as we would very soon see.

Now inside Bethlehem, off we went to the designated *rendezvous*, the Paradise Hotel, just past Rachel's Tomb. The hotel had been closed for six months, which is not too surprising since Palestinian gunmen of the *Tanzim* militia have used the roof for firing at the IDF at Rachel's Tomb, which has been an Israeli Army Fortress for some time. Since the Norwegians were not asking about making reservations at the Paradise, I decided not to bore them with details about *Tanzim* forays and IDF counter fire. A brisk wind was just coming up out of the north, which was a great excuse to invite everyone to nip around the corner to a sheltered spot in a back street.

More marchers joined us at the Paradise, and many faces were familiar. A handful of Christian Peacemaker Team people from Hebron appeared, wearing their red CPT caps. My American companions quickly made friends, reminiscing with the older CPT gray-haired and athletic types about civil rights marches in the American South in the 60s.

The Italian contingent and the Rapprochement Palestinians arrived together from Beit Sahour, with plenty of signs in several languages. The Rapprochement founder, Ghassan, led the group with his colleague George, accompanied by the other George and the third George (Christian Palestinians are all called George). With them was Jad, a veteran nonviolent activist who headed the "*Intifada* Agriculture" movement in the 80s, and was jailed by the Israeli Army for growing tomatoes in defiance of military regulations.

A ripple of excitement moved through the gathering with the arrival of the much-loved Abuna Ibrahim – "Father Abraham" –

a stooped Arab priest in a simple black cassock, who had seen many years of struggle for Palestinian liberation.

The ex-pats were mostly unaware of the quiet presence of one or two Israeli citizens in the group, activists who had made their way around the checkpoint to the Palestinian side. Army protocols were harsh on Israelis who breached the code to stand beside Palestinians; these marchers had taken some serious risks and were essential to the plan. Mobile phones in hand, they were in constant contact with the Israeli contingent on the Jerusalem road. The respect and deference that the Palestinian organizers showed their Israeli colleagues was heart-warming.

At a strategy meeting the day before, I had agreed to print out some "free bus passes" that we planned to give the Israeli soldiers. These "tickets" bore the following Good News.

> *Israeli Soldier! The Occupation is Over! You Can Go Home! Please Take the Next Bus Home and Live in Peace!*

We decided that we would offer to pay the bus fare if any soldier looked interested. I had produced over 150 of these "vouchers," and although there were certainly not that many soldiers at the checkpoint, the vouchers were all gone very soon. I suspect that some of the marchers could not resist pocketing a few as souvenirs.

We were all gathered. The march began.

As we rounded the corner of the Paradise and headed north toward the checkpoint, I took some deep breaths to calm the flutter in my nether regions. The banners unfurled with their messages – all of them calling for justice, nonviolence and an end to the Occupation. Hesitant at first, the Norwegians soon had their little red and blue flags out and were right in step. The Rapprochement folks were close to the front, Ghassan and Jad wearing impeccable suits, and Abuna Ibrahim in his black cassock and broad-brimmed clerical hat.

Women – both local and ex-pats – were linking arms along the front line of our march. We had discussed the importance of women's presence up front, on the assumption that soldiers in general do not have much experience confronting them, at least not in a civil disobedience context. This turned out to be absolutely correct.

Walking in orderly lines stretched right across the road, we approached Rachel's Tomb, with its towering IDF fortification built around the dubious shrine. The biblical matriarch would have turned over in her grave to see her children gathering there, but we didn't. As the glint of army sniper scopes tracked us, we about-faced, turned our back on the matriarchal tomb and took the Caritas Road. The checkpoint was our goal, and on we went.

Camera people scurried along with us as we rounded another corner and walked into the first of three checkpoint stations. The soldiers were right there, and we all stopped. The officer in charge informed us that we could go through to the next point, but there we would have to stop. We all walked on. By this time we were all linking arms, singing *"We Shall Overcome."* A verse of the Palestinian freedom song *"Biladi Biladi"* wasn't as successful, since the ex-pats didn't know the words. At the second checkpoint, a serious cordon of soldiers awaited us. We moved forward in a broad line, with plenty of women in front. And then we moved up close. The stand-off began.

"Up close" was a strategy, not an accident. We had discussed the advantages of close contact, even to the point of physically touching the soldiers. This was one of the most interesting aspects of this march. Standing right there, nose to nose with the soldiers, we could look into their eyes, into their pockets, into their motives, into their hearts – and they, if they wished, could look into ours. We were actually so close they could not lift their guns, even if they had wanted to. Also, with all those women right up against them, the soldiers were, clearly, a bit embarrassed, but also just a bit excited. This was not at all a bad thing. It seems that adrenaline (or another hormone?) has a hard time running in two directions at once.

At one point, all the marchers in the front line raised hands above their heads. The gesture was not one of submission, but rather a symbolic image which evoked an immediate association: "We are surrounded by soldiers with guns, we look imprisoned, but our spirit is free!" And, most importantly, this gesture said. "We are not holding weapons, we are not here to hurt you!"

At another point, when the officer in charge said something about arrests, we all took the cue from our appointed monitors, and sat down, arms entwined. This too was very effective. You could tell it was making the soldiers nervous to have us at their feet, all linked together. It was going to be extremely difficult to arrest the whole clump.

The details of nonviolent action are familiar. They served civil rights marchers in the USA forty years ago, and they still work. We were recycling tactics used in the voters' rights marches in the 60s: the sit-down and the gentle body-push. Soldiers are briefed on handling violent confrontations from a distance, with tear gas, stun grenades, steel bullets with rubber coating, and live ammunition. None of these are practical against a group of demonstrators sitting at your very feet, or pushing up against you (gently of course!) with their bodies.

I had handed out all my symbolic "free bus tickets" and chatted with as many of the soldiers as I could, in both Hebrew and English, taking advantage of every angle, getting their attention and making eye contact. The same was happening up and down the line. Then, gradually, and without using our hands, we gently pushed forward into the soldiers' line. They pushed back, of course, but not too hard. Here and there, an over-zealous marcher pushed aggressively, and I noticed a French guy right next to me getting red in the face. His hand had been scratched by the soldier's gun as they grappled, and the smear of blood on the marcher's finger was a reminder, a warning. I put my arm through his, made eye contact, and asked him if he was okay. He thought my French was pretty silly, and that broke the ice. Things calmed down.

Right along the line, our little dance was going on – absurd but serious; there was conversation, photos were taken, reporters were interviewing. The monitors of the march were in conversation with the officer in charge, who had radioed for police backup. The soldiers themselves were not supposed to make any civil arrests of internationals, which is why the police had been summoned. Of course, we hoped to move right up to the checkpoint before they arrived.

We also knew that the Israeli activist group, north of us, was lined up facing another soldier cordon on the Jerusalem side. They were using the same tactics, and the two cordons were gradually being pushed closer and closer. It wasn't more than half an hour before the officer in charge allowed a "small delegation" of Israelis to pass through to meet the Palestinians. This worked like a key in a ponderous lock, as the Israeli delegation walked forward, now in full view of all of us on the Palestinian side of the checkpoint.

Meanwhile, "our" army cordon had been slowly moving back to accommodate our ebb and flow. It took only a glimpse of the approaching Israeli "delegates" to make it impossible for our forward movement to be stopped. Soldiers' resistance to our pressure became half-hearted as cheerful Hebrew greetings filled the air. We simply walked through the checkpoint, hands meeting hands, hugs all around, cries of "Shalom!" and "Salamat," Hebrew mingling now with Arabic and Italian and Norwegian and French and English and Danish and all the rest.

A union of some kind was reached that day. Who knows what history will make of it? To me this union seemed to be gained through courage but without anger (well, at least with a disciplined anger!). It was organic but logical, benevolent but not overly controlled. I don't really remember exactly how the soldiers regrouped in one last vain effort to prevent the Palestinians from joining their Israeli friends waiting for them beyond the checkpoint. Familiar faces of the Israeli "critical left" were all around us. There was a wave of relief mixed with elation, and a strange sadness too. The checkpoint was still standing – for we had not intended to dismantle it by force. The Occupation was still very much intact, for its removal requires a greater strength than simple determination can provide, and a union and a wisdom not yet ours to call upon.

"Somewhere, ages and ages hence / I shall be telling this with a sigh…" so wrote Robert Frost. Would those of us who marched that day look back on our decisions with the poet's clarity? We took a "road less traveled" – but would that make "all the difference"? Would it make any difference at all? How could we know what seeds our actions would sow? Soon, we parted again, Palestinians to their hopes and their frustrations within the confines of Occupation, internationals to their thoughtful freedoms, Israelis to their uneasy state in between on the moral low ground, compromised by too much power and too little compassion.

We went our separate paths, but we were together. On that Holy Saturday, for those hard-earned minutes at the Bethlehem checkpoint, we were together. And it was beautiful.

PERFECTLY SAFE RUBBLE
Jerusalem, 28th May 2001

The scenes of devastation from the wedding hall disaster in West Jerusalem are staring us in the face. Our fascination for horror makes us gaze and gaze, and finally ask "Why them?" and "Why not me?" We look, but will soon forget. The nuances of this tragedy are subtle, and they will evade us, unless we stop to think. Here are messages, images that might awaken us, metaphors that might challenge us. But we prefer the familiar ghoulishness of our shocked senses struggling with generic and meaningless human suffering. Still, the deeper voices will not go away... Like the silent screams of victims under layers of concrete, they will haunt us until we speak their names, until we reach out our hands... and even then.

Late on the night of May 24th, on the third floor of the *Versailles* wedding hall, Keren and Assi danced with their guests. When the floor caved in, twenty-four died, hundreds were injured, but the bride and groom survived. The dust had not yet settled, and I could already hear the hissing of the impossible questions. Why did this happen? What did they do wrong? Is there a dreadful divine logic to sorrow and pain?

"Why do terrible things happen to innocent people?" The dreadful logical answer (how attractive it sometimes is!) is that they don't. If someone suffers, someone is guilty. We have enough kooks and fanatics to keep that travesty of human thought current. I can just hear them now: "Aha! God can still punish! Israelis have bombed Palestinian homes and public buildings into piles of rubble, now let them know what rubble feels like!"

Many years ago, a Galilean Rabbi heard that a tower in Jerusalem had collapsed, killing eighteen. He heard the hiss of the dreadful logic: bad things happen to bad people! He did not agree, so he said: "Do you think that these folks were worse sinners than all the other people living in Jerusalem? No!"

At this point the Galilean Rabbi had made his point: decent people suffer, accidents happen. But then he went on, adding a cryptic warning: "But unless you repent, you will all perish like this!" Ouch. What on earth?

Accidents happen; there is no need of a vengeful God for that. But accidents begin to have meaning when you stop to think about them. Disaster strikes? So, think about it. Be changed by it. Turn yourself around by it. Don't just blame somebody and forget it. This is *your* tower, *your* wedding hall, *your* life.

The theological question of whether God treats us justly is called "theodicy." The "tit-for-tat" version has been around for a long time. In the biblical Book of Job, "Job's comforters" (actually they are his torturers!) try to tell him that he is having a horrendous life because he is a horrendous person. The whole point of the Book of Job is to develop the awareness that this is nonsense. Good people often suffer; bad people are often blessed. And Job's God thunders from the whirlwind: "What is, *is*. Deal with it!"

Think about it (says the Voice from the Storm) this way: you can no more change reality than you can stop the dawn or the earthquake. The only question is: will you live in this knowledge, or will you curse God, and die? Response is everything.

Let me invite you for a tour of Jerusalem's theodicy workshop after the wedding hall disaster. Let's look at some responses. Here is Exhibit A, a news release printed in *Haaretz:*

> The Palestinian Authority expresses its deep
> condolences to the State [of Israel] and the Israeli
> people for the victims of the wedding hall [disaster].
> The [Palestinian] leadership has given immediate
> instruction to the department of civil defense to
> offer help to their Israeli counterparts to assist in
> rescue operations.

The "civil defense," no less. Would that be the Palestinian police confined to Hebron and Jericho, or perhaps the militias with guns who are shooting at Israeli settlements (as the Israeli "civil defense" asserts) and subsequently being bombed into the Stone Age by Israeli pilots or assassinated with rockets from Apache helicopters? The mind boggles, and that is par for the theodicy course.

The Palestinian Authority news release may go down in history as one of the most generous, or most ironic, diplomatic initiatives ever conceived. But it sure beats the sick theodicy of the Orthodox Jewish leaders who are saying that Keren and Assi were sinners, heretics, or worse, and brought this disaster upon themselves. I am sure Job would have preferred Palestinian political irony to religious self-righteousness.

Now let us look at Exhibit B. A British radio report tells us that the families of Keren and Assi originally planned to celebrate the wedding in an Israeli settlement in the Occupied Territories. They decided against this, however, fearing that guests would be attacked by Palestinians while *en route* to the wedding. Everyone knows how dangerous Arabs can be, so it's safer to take refuge from "the situation" in Jewish West Jerusalem, where you can be safe. Of course, once-upon-a-time Arabs lived in West Jerusalem too, but that was sorted out years ago. No Arabs, no problems, right?

It's amazing to find out why Israelis get married these days. Exhibit C is London's *Sunday Observer*, where Suzanne Goldberg writes that the wedding "was meant as an escape from the daily stresses of suicide bombs and drive-by shootings during the last eight months of a Palestinian uprising." Poor Israelis. Can't those terrorists even let them get married in peace? And of course, when the floor crashed down, the first thought that came to every mind was that a terrorist bomb had exploded. It was not a terrorist attack, this time. But, it certainly could have been, and that's what counts.

A score of Jewish deaths, but terrorists didn't do it. Who then is responsible for the death, the broken dreams, the terrible injuries, the trauma? Exhibit D: here are a few candidates, all under arrest in Jerusalem's police station: (1) the owners of the hall (Israelis), just trying to make a profit by removing a few concrete pillars so they can crowd in more (Israeli) revelers; (2) the (Israeli) contractors who poured the concrete floor and thought it was okay to use sub-standard "thin, sandy concrete laid over iron mesh"; (3) the (Israeli) inventor of that brilliant cost-effective technique, who said on Israeli radio that it's "perfectly safe." They are all under arrest.

Israelis don't need a vengeful God or a hateful terrorist to hurt them; it turns out they can cause each other a lot of pain without outside help. But there is little comfort in knowing this, for what can be done about it? Are you wishing, maybe, just maybe, that it *had* been a terrorist attack? At least then the Air Force could bomb Ramallah, and we would all feel better, right?

We are about to turn away, sobered and baffled by Jerusalem's version of "Bad Things Happen." But before we give up, before we leave poor Keren and Assi with their sad, accidental and potentially meaningless disaster, let's see just one more little item, one we were very likely to miss.

Exhibit E.

On Saturday, we read in the *Daily Telegraph*, "rescuers promise to keep working for five days to sift the rubble" for survivors. Fair enough. People under rubble have been known to stay alive a long time. The rabbis in Israel have given their dispensation to work through the Sabbath (who, I can't help but wonder, was actually waiting for their permission? The question won't go away) – so everyone is doing everything they possibly can.

Now we come to Sunday's *London Observer*. It is May 27th, barely three days since the disaster, and the "perfectly safe" rubble of the wedding hall is growing cold. In fact, the search for survivors has been called off.

Called off? Why so soon? A perfectly good reason: the army man in charge, IDF Colonel David, says that the 620 wedding guests are all accounted for. Twenty-four dead, the rest injured or spared, all accounted for. Thank goodness. We can stop digging and turn our energy to suing the contractors!

But wait. What's this?

> Workers still feared trapped in rubble... The bodies of foreign or Palestinian workers employed in an aluminum factory on the first floor of the [wedding hall] in Jewish west Jerusalem could be trapped beneath the rubble.

Excuse me? Those damn terrorists again? No, no, stupid! Workers. But not Jewish workers. Maybe Thai workers, or Ghanian workers, sleeping on the factory floor, who knows why? Or... maybe Palestinian workers, shadowy illegals without permits, staying in the factory by night, keeping out of trouble from the Border Patrol.

Workers, 'still feared trapped in rubble.' So...why is the rescue operation being called off? Barely three days have passed. They might still be alive!

Oh, yes. Well...you see...this *is* 'Jewish west Jerusalem,' you know. It says so right here. Palestinian workers, well... It would be illegal for them to sleep in West Jerusalem, you know. And besides, if they did, they are probably already dead. Or maybe they aren't even there. The important thing is that the guests are all accounted for. If there is anyone else in the rubble, it's certainly not Jewish wedding guests. Right?

With the real people all accounted for, the rubble is perfectly safe.

As I write this, no one knows the fate of the 'workers.' Nameless and uninvited, entombed in concrete, are they still screaming for their enemies to remember them and have mercy? Is this some dreadful medieval proof of God's retribution, or a meaningless blip on the human screen, something we can say "tut-tut" about and turn away from, forget about? Neither. This is our rubble, and our responsibility.

It can only get more ugly, the deeper we dare to dig. The rickety wedding hall is still with us. The floor, hastily thrown on an ideological mesh, is still bending under our insane celebrations, ready to crack. The dancers, young and innocent, are victims of their own ignorance, deliberate and otherwise. They are betrayed by the greed of their fat and prosperous leaders. The guests have been duped to think they are safe from terror and loss, but the first to die will be the last to deserve it. And deep down, beneath our "normal" lives, in the underworld of our victorious and rave-driven society, the dispossessed are dying, and determined not to die alone.

How does Annie Lennox put it? *Accidents speak louder than words.* But only if someone is alive enough, serious enough, human enough, to listen.

BOTH SIDES NOW
Jerusalem, 24th July 2001

Through July the spiral of violence spins on. Two Israeli soldiers are killed at a bus stop by a suicide bomber in Binyamina. Four Palestinians are assassinated by Israeli helicopter fire in Bethlehem. A Palestinian family is murdered by settler gunfire as they drive down the road near Hebron. The names blur, the incidents interface. There are radio cover-ups and advertisements of normalcy: "Ceasefire," "Cooling Off Period," "International Observer Force" – all slogans, no substance. The killing in the Holy Land goes on at a hellish pace.

Early in the morning on July 18th my daughter Moriah was inducted into the Israeli Army. For months the date loomed, the event slowly took on the quality of something real. Resisted, argued, discussed, cried over, yelled about, denied, rejected, embraced, planned and unplanned for – now real. My daughter, my only daughter, my little girl, is in the uniform of the IDF. Her heart, her body, her conscience, clothed in a moving target. Her days, her actions, her knowledge, her dreams, her weaknesses and her strengths, enclosed in the hugely powerful war machine of a military state under a dubious leadership, committed to an increasingly brutal policy of Occupation and Separation. My daughter is an Israeli soldier.

In my many conversations with Mori, I struggled with her about her choice, her path. I did the research on conscientious objection (such as it is in Israel – which isn't much). I brought her piles of information from the human rights organizations. I told her about Sharon and Sabra and Shatilla, about Barak and the Oslo illusions, and about war crimes and the evils we are all part of. I told her of my hours with the tiny Palestinian and Israeli nonviolent resistance movement, my visits to bombarded homes, the havoc wreaked by the armed settler gangs, the glowering presence of the military posts overlooking the homes of Beit Sahour and Ramallah, the desperate demonstrations at the barricades, the confrontations with the border patrols and the settler militias, the repeated scenarios of force and weakness, the tear gas grenades tossed, the guns pointed, the jeeps growling... Everything I described was profoundly personal, touched us here, where we stand, on both sides now.

I sketched in my words the impossible but possible: Moriah in uniform on one side of the Occupation checkpoint, myself in a resistance demonstration on the other. "What if...? What if...?" "Dad, it won't happen." "Mori, nothing is impossible. Just think about it. What if?"

We talked and cried and laughed, we drank numberless cups of coffee and we told our stories again and again. Moriah described the sense of belonging she feels, the bond with her Israeli friends and classmates, her unwillingness to leave them behind, to turn away from them, to deny her Israeliness, to fly out of here. She spoke of the frustration she feels at her country's wrong policies, the Occupation, the destruction of a whole generation's hope for peace and justice and a normal life. She spoke with anger, but with courage too. She, too, described the indescribable: the opportunity to work from within, to counsel and direct and be a voice of reason and conscience. She was choosing freely the role she would play in uniform, the course in social work she would take, the non-commissioned officer status she would reach, the way to be a force for good...

I looked into her eyes, and they were clear. She grew, and every moment a new facet of herself was outlined in the strong Jerusalem light. Her beauty and her honesty shone through the tears. She graduated from high school, she danced on the stage of her childhood one last time. She bought a knapsack and said she was going to Greece with her buddies. Then they backed out and she stayed at home. She got a haircut and we read together the last chapters of *The Princess and the Goblin*. I gave her my old guitar and she asked me to teach her to play *Bo Jangles*. Still we talked and argued. Then, inexorably, it was July.

On July 18th, at the IDF mustering point in West Jerusalem, Moriah was inducted. She asked for us to be there; she couldn't have kept us away. On that day, I was not a teacher or a theologian or a guide, or an advocate or activist. I was just an *Abba* like every other *Abba* there. Mori's mother and I stood together, closer than I can remember we have stood since the divorce. Jonathan played the role of teenage brother perfectly, with just the right balance of cool and warmth. Jesse, upset, decided to stay at home, then wished he hadn't... We were simply there, to say goodbye to Moriah, to echo the words of the Hebrew song: *Take wing...and take good care.*

Mori's classmates showed up too to see her off, and we all clustered around her in the parking lot where the big buses stood. There were a hundred young women – it was women's induction day – all dressed up, all gorgeous, all with designer shades and mobile phones and smart new knapsacks. Big hugs, some tears, some laughter. I slipped into Mori's bag a little box of my homemade "*intifada* chip cookies" and pinned an Irish shamrock talisman to her hem. Then we all hugged her, and Mori left us. She stood briefly in line, picked up her army unit file, shouldered her pack, and joined the other girls on the bus. And suddenly, of course, they were not girls any more – they were women, and soldiers. The bus pulled out of the lot, and Mori's face behind the glass disappeared, but her hand was still visible, waving, waving.

The next time I see Moriah, she will be in the uniform of the Army of the Occupation.

My mind is reeling. How is it possible for two worlds to meet like this without an explosion? How can I find my way in this impossible maze of emotions? Who will keep us together? Who will prevent the realities of the Occupation, of the confrontations all around us, of the fears and passions of this poor land, from separating us? Parents from their children, brother from sister, a daughter from her father? Even if no one can prevent this, God help us, can we not at least admit that it hurts us deeply? Can't we at least recognize that we are not the only ones being hurt, and try to tell the story of the two sides of every pain?

The Buddhist teacher Thich Nhat Hanh writes of this moment:

> To reconcile conflicting parties, we must have the ability to understand the suffering of both sides. If we take sides, it is impossible to do the work of reconciliation. And humans want to take sides... Are there people who are still available to both sides? They need not do much. They need only do one thing: go to one side and tell all about the suffering endured by the other side, and go to the other side and tell all about the suffering endured by this side. That is our chance for peace... But how many of us are able to do that?

How many? I open my hand, Mori, and let go of yours. Here where I stand on the threshold between warring worlds, I watch you fly away from me, and my eyes follow until they can no longer see you through the window flashing in the sun, and then my heart goes further still. I thought to hide you in this threshold place, Jerusalem, to protect you from its wounds. But this is now your place, yours too. East and West, child and woman, right and wrong, Israel and Palestine, hope and fear and courage and justice – they all meet in your story – both sides now.

Tell it well.

WHAT ABOUT THE KIDS?
Jerusalem, 30th September 2001

On Thursday, September 20th, a young mother named Sarit Amrani was mortally wounded by Palestinian gunmen on the road to the settlement in the West Bank where she and her family lived. As the attackers raked the car with bullets, Sarit's husband was badly hurt, but – according to the newspaper report – "their three young children, two toddlers and a 3-month-old infant, escaped the attack with no injuries."

I don't think so.

When Nidal Abu-Salamah takes his old furniture truck through the IDF checkpoints in the Jordan Valley, the army will not let him through if he is alone – they suspect he might be a terrorist. So he takes his children with him. Fathi, aged 6, and Nur, aged 5, miss a lot of school, because their father is often turned back at gunpoint at the checkpoint, and has to try again and again to get his furniture to market. Nidal's kids see the abuse by the soldiers, the humiliation and the fear in their father's eyes, day after day, from their perch in the hot and dusty truck cab. And they are the lucky ones. At least their house is still standing when they finally get home.

God only knows what kind of trauma and long-term damage is done to children in this confrontation. We are all too ready to give our attention to eloquent adult expressions of rage and grief, but the silent scream of the very young goes unheard. And yet, if there is any hope for anyone at all in this long-running battle between Jews and Arabs, it is the young children who might, just might, have a chance to see that hope become real.

So...what about the kids?

During the past year, since the beginning of the present *Intifada*, over 547 Palestinians have been killed, including Palestinians killed within Israel. This includes 432 civilians killed by Israeli security forces, 13 killed by the police (in Nazareth), and 11 civilians killed by Israeli civilians (settlers). The remaining 91 were Palestinian security forces killed in combat with the IDF. In other words, in this war, only 20% of the Palestinians killed were actual combatants in the accepted sense of the word. "Collateral damage" of 80% is not a good figure, no matter what any army says.

Israelis have also been killed – 171 as of September 14th. Their names appear with short tributes in each day's *Jerusalem Post*. Over half of the dead were civilians. "Collateral damage" of 50% is not a good figure either. If this is a war, it is a very dirty one.

What about the kids?

On the Israeli side, the dead include: four 17-year-olds, two boys and six girls aged 16, three girls and a boy aged 15, two boys and a girl aged 14, a boy of 13, a girl of 10, a girl of 8, a boy of 4, a boy of 2, a 10-month-old baby girl and a 5-month-old baby boy. Twenty-six children aged 17 and younger, some killed by Palestinian attackers within Israel and some in attacks on Jewish settlement targets in the Occupied Territories of the West Bank and Gaza.

Twenty-six young lives cut short is a heavy toll. But the real accounting cannot begin until we look at the Palestinian kids as well. Here are the *B'tselem* Human Rights Organization figures for September 12th: 127 Palestinian children aged 17 and younger have been killed. Twenty-eight 17-year olds, twenty-four 16-year olds, twenty-five 15-year-olds, twenty-three 14-year-olds, ten 13-year-olds, seven 12-year-olds, three 11-year-olds, two 10-year-olds, two 9-year-olds, two 8-year-olds, and a 4-month-old baby girl.

The older of these kids were sometimes armed with stones and slingshots. They were shot dead during confrontations with Israeli soldiers. Others were killed at a distance by army snipers.

In addition, a 2-month-old baby Palestinian girl was killed by Israeli settlers, and a 12-year-old Palestinian boy was accidentally shot by Palestinians when Palestinian civilians tried to stop the gunmen from shooting at an IDF post.

My mind cannot grasp all this. How is it humanly possible for adults, no matter how conflicted, to kill, at such close range, so many children? Isn't there some kind of built-in safety catch, an evolutionary taboo that would tear the finger from the trigger? I don't get it. I can only come up with the middle-class middle-of-the-road complaint: "What were those poor kids doing there in the first place?" In other words, I want to blame the parents: how can grown-ups allow their children to become victims? Then, still incredulous, I come up with an even less impressive rhetorical question: "What on earth can I do about it?"

Good question.

An email arrived today from an Israeli peace activist in a Palestinian village in the West Bank:

> Another example of life under Occupation that
> doesn't make headlines. Billal Muhamed Akel is
> fourteen years old. This evening...he was beaten,
> as his parents watched helplessly, and taken
> away by Israeli soldiers. His whereabouts are
> still unknown. The soldiers said they knew the
> boy had not been throwing stones, but they beat
> him and kidnapped him so that he would tell
> them who *was* throwing stones...

I just had to file it and move on – what else could I do?

Even if a miracle happens and the army returns Billal to his home tonight, he is already deeply injured. The wound is there, unseen, in every child I can see around me, Jew or Christian or Muslim, Israeli or Palestinian or both. Some hide it better, some are tough and glib, but all are torn and bruised. "Jew or Arab," "occupied or occupiers," "victors and victims" – these are the roles the grown-ups play. For the kids, there is only the wounding.

I ask you: what about the kids?

AS IF
Jerusalem, 4th October 2001

An ad in a local Israeli paper catches my eye just before *Rosh HaShana*: "Celebrate in Israel, and feel as if you're abroad!" This is interesting. Why would Israelis want to celebrate the New Year in Israel while feeling as if they were in, say, New York? Considering recent events "abroad," one might think most Israelis would prefer observing the Jewish Holidays at home. Isn't the Jewish homeland a much safer place to celebrate the holidays? So what is all this "as if..."?

The atmosphere of dissemblance has become thick enough to choke us, and still we go on with our celebrations. When the Jerusalem municipality set off fireworks to usher in the holidays near the walls of the Old City, it was natural that some of us flinched, wondering if the IDF was launching rockets at Abu Tor. Just a few days ago, under heavy security guard, thousands of Israeli citizens marched into a green municipal park, waving blue and white flags and playing patriotic music. Meanwhile, during the Jewish High Holy Days, Palestinians in the refugee camp of Shu'afat, just a few miles away, and still inside the Jerusalem municipal lines, watched as fourteen of their homes were destroyed by army bulldozers. In days of awe, in times of shame like these, what kind of pride or comfort in their nation can even the most patriotic of Israelis feel? Is this why so many Israelis are choosing, discreetly, to go "abroad"?

This is not just a local story anymore. We are all "as if" abroad, all the time, even if we play house in the "security" of our back yard. To understand the extent to which we are deceiving ourselves, listen closely to the gossip in the global village. Just a few weeks ago – it seems a century ago! – terrorist attacks in West Jerusalem might have seemed to the average American like disturbing but distant distractions from normal life. Suddenly, "responding to terrorism" is the relevant buzz-word. Just a few weeks ago, Israel's "elimination" of Palestinian leaders, with American weapons, and in broad daylight, might have struck the average New Yorker as a rather exotic example of foreign policy. Now the whole world seems divided between those trying to "take out" bin Laden and those trying to keep him in. "Retaliation" is firmly entered into the lexicon of universal virtues.

As soon as he heard of the September 11th terrorist attacks on the Twin Towers, a construction worker in Vermont summed it up: "Somebody pays for this. Someone's got to pay." Indeed. But who? Even as the combined technological might of America and Britain is bombing Afghanistan around the clock transforming mud huts into rough little molehills in the desert and killing civilians, many of us are still swallowing new versions of the "might makes right" philosophy that has seduced us for so long. For all our talk of a "war on evil," we just want someone to pay. As if that would make us feel safe. Since September 11th, we have had some time to think this through. How are we doing? Are we getting beyond vengeance to a glimmer of wisdom?

A week before the 9/11 atrocities, an article by Fouad Ajami warned that the "path of the martyrs," the glorification of religiously motivated suicidal terrorism, is leading Palestinians further and further from freedom. Of course it is important to decry the folly of viewing "suicide martyrs" as heroes. And yet, Ajami's warning was not as courageous as it needed to be. It still could not answer the essential question: "Why do they do it?"

"Why *really* do they hate us?" This is a question that could only be dragged out of us by the shock of a brutal run-in with the truth. Ajami attributes Palestinian terrorism to "furious envy" of Israeli prosperity, as if hundreds of youths from Jenin and Nablus and Gaza could be willing to destroy themselves and others simply because they are jealous of people with swimming pools in Tel Aviv. Ajami's article never mentions the one word that truth requires: "humiliation." In the midst of a potentially important message, Ajami simply stops short, unwilling to give the hatred a real name.

And now, a full month after the Twin Towers fell, are we any closer to being ready for truth? Yes, and no. At least, we now see that Israel's moral dilemma is not unique; terrorists don't just hate Jews. Israelis, however, can hardly celebrate this revelation. Rather than passing the buck, they should be among the first to seek the reasons for hatred, and to address those reasons with social change. Jewish history is filled with the cries of hatred's victims, and the plea not to forget. If six million Jews and millions of other ethnic minorities could be wiped out, deemed "subhuman," by a Nazi regime sure of its moral superiority, and if the founding of the State of Israel is some kind of redemption for the remnant that remain, the question "Why do they hate us?" is relevant to Israeli society. Israelis (and Americans too) would do well to be more concerned about finding the reasons for hatred, rather than acting as if it is an alien phenomenon, a murderous but mindless scourge.

Not to ask *Why?* is to cling to innocence. Too many Israelis (and Americans, among others) are choosing innocence over truth – as if it ended there.

Unbounded hatred is not something individuals should have to bear alone; societies have responsibilities. When Hila Hershkovitz lost her husband in a Palestinian terrorist shooting in the Jordan Valley, she and her two children took a break from their life in an Israeli settlement to visit her family in London. "It was nice to get away to a place where no one shoots at you and no one tries to blow you up as you stand at a bus stop," she said. On the flight back to Israel, reality kicked in. "When I saw the lights of Tel Aviv from the plane window I began to cry and thought, what are we coming back to?"

A heart-rending question, especially since Hila seems so alone in asking it. Her society, which for decades has been preaching an Israeli manifest destiny of forcibly colonizing the Jordan Valley (as well as the rest of the West Bank), can offer Hila false innocence, condolences and loans, but not answers. And so, not once does she allow herself the real question: "Why was my husband killed?"

Or does this question have only one answer? "They hate us, not for any wrong we have done them, not for any suffering that may have broken them, not for any reason we can ever understand, but simply because we are who we are. We are Jewish, they are not. We are free, they are not. We are modern, they are not. We are prosperous, they are not. We are good and normal people, and they are evil hateful mutants. This is why they hate us."

As if this line is anything like good enough. Citizens need wisdom from their leaders, society needs truth. We cannot build futures on yesterday's prejudice. Generations of Israelis have been taught that Arabs hate them – are Americans now going to follow suit? Golda Meir's famous dictum – "We can never forgive the Arabs for forcing us to kill their children" – has all the pathos, all the obtuseness, all the righteousness, of a full-fledged falsehood. Such falsehoods work for so long, as self-fulfilling scenarios, that they finally are hailed as truth. Now, generals bombing Afghanistan will quote Golda. Is this an answer?

I don't see much evidence that Israeli public wisdom is ready for the big question. Even as American and British planes drop punitive ordinance on – let's face it – victims of an "as if" new world order, Israeli voices play on the deepest fears of local "innocents." A chilling essay in *Haaretz* on October 12th is as belligerent as anything from Washington or Kabul. "The enemies of the West," writes Avi Shavit, are "the new evil." They are "the new Saladins," and the "tenacity of their faith in their god (sic!)...[has] transformed them into...the enemies of life itself."

Once upon a time we learned to our astonishment from the poet/singer Sting that our old demons, the Russian Soviets, "love their children too." Not so "the new enemies," the purveyors of this "new evil." They do not love their children. Their "god" is spelled with a small "g." And they are beyond the pale.

This is the nightmare of *Independence Day*, a Hollywood blockbuster that some sensitive soul may now be regretting the making of. Humanity is threatened by sophisticated aliens, who show nothing but cruel loathing for their human prey. America's cities crumble like card houses. The only catharsis this film can offer is the farcical scene of Israeli and Arab fighter pilots joining cause with mighty America against the alien menace, and the final annihilation of the alien spaceship by a courageous suicide mission. It all rings absurdly false, and suddenly we are living it.

It is still so fresh, the shock still makes us tremble. 285 million Americans mourn the death of 3000 innocent victims of the terror attacks on the World Trade Towers and the Pentagon. Such a loss in one day is inconceivable, surpasses all measure, all comparison. It is as if such suffering could have been inflicted only by a mutant strain, not by ordinary mortals. It is a *sui generis* suffering. Or is it?

From September 1940 to June 1941, less than one year, the German Luftwaffe dropped 18,000 tons of high explosives on English cities, killing 40,000 civilians – men, women and children. I know a man who was a child in London then, and he reminds me that when the United States finally entered the war, revenge was quick. "We made the German raids on England look like small potatoes. We turned Dresden into an inferno of fire... Did it make us feel any better? Did it bring meaning out of the insanity? Actually, it did not... Nor did it bring back one of [the dead], not even one child."

Some years after the war, German and English teenagers embraced and wept in the ruins left by their parents' hatred. Not then, and not since, have the victims of all that slaughter been taught to think that their enemies lacked love for their children, or hated life itself.

There is no "new evil." The world has not changed after September 11th, although our vision has. If our perception is that those who hate us can be nothing but godless and heartless subhumans, then we need to search the mirror of our own actions. For such a mirror, Israeli society does not need to look far.

There are around 3 million Palestinians living under Israeli Occupation in the West Bank and Gaza, and they have lost 600 precious lives in the last year, many of them children. Percentages mean nothing to the heart. So, just stop a minute, if you are one of the 285,000,000 Americans who might read this, and imagine, if you can, that 57,000 Americans have been shot dead, over the last year. That's the equivalent. How would that kind of shock and mourning feel?

Can we imagine a human being enduring loss and humiliation, being filled with rage, becoming a terrorist, committing mass murder – and still remaining human? Or is that a privilege we reserve only for history's victors who drop mass death on Dresden, atomic holocaust on Japan, liquid fire on Asia, or "smart" bombs on the Middle East? We, too, have sinned.

Little yellow bags of American food rations in the Afghan desert, small groups of Israelis rebuilding Palestinian homes, these are tiny symbols of the campaign we really need, not a campaign of righteous wrath but of repentance and decisive change. It is time to ask where terrorism comes from, not just where it is going. Only then will we know what to do about it.

> The means may be likened to a seed, the end to a tree: and there is just the same inviolable connection between the means and the end as there is between the seed and the tree.

Gandhi had it right. If our means to fight evil is to terrorize others, then terror will be our end.

As if we didn't know.

OLIVE TREES
Jerusalem, 18th November 2001

Yesterday I crossed the lines to visit the olive trees.

A journalist friend had asked me to accompany him to the middle of the West Bank Palestinian Territories, where a group of Israeli activists are helping Palestinian farmers harvest their olive crop. I was to be a translator of sorts, and a witness as well. We left Jerusalem and headed north, in a car with a press permit, through IDF road blocks and checkpoints, into a land covered with olive trees.

In the present conflict situation, what do olive trees have to do with anything? One of the oldest symbols of peace, the olive branch is looking bedraggled these days. But olives are practically the only source of income the Palestinian villagers have, since they can't cross the checkpoints into Israel to work, and can't sell vegetables in the markets due to military closures. Violence in the cities of Ramallah and Jericho, Nablus and Bethlehem has destroyed the Palestinian tourist economy. At least folks can harvest the olive crop on the last few acres of groves not already expropriated by the settlement movements to construct Israeli villas. And if the villagers can harvest their crop, they'll have some olive oil to sell and olives to use as food.

There is one big problem. A constant state of conflict exists along the roads, and spills over into the fields as well. Travel is harder and harder as the army cracks down, demanding permits to move from village to village. To make matters worse, in olive groves adjacent to Israeli settlements, the settler committees have obtained permission from the army to prevent villagers from entering the groves "for security reasons." In addition, hundreds of trees, some of them very old, have been uprooted and bulldozed out of the way where the settlers have told the army that there is a danger of Palestinians throwing stones at passing settler cars. When villagers come to their groves, they do not know whether they might find gangs of armed settlers there, ready to drive them off. In short, the harvest has become a complex challenge. And the olives are maturing quickly. Soon they will drop and rot.

We drive fast, bypassing Ramallah and continuing through the valley of Lebonah. Here, in the ancient biblical tale, the sons of Benjamin hid in the vineyards and lay in lusty wait to carry off the girls of Shiloh. Here, in the twenty-first century, teenage Arab boys wait for the Israelis, and stone their cars. Up on the ridge we glimpse a running skirmish, as young Palestinians leap along the rooftops of the village of Sinjil, slinging stones at an Israeli patrol. The acrid whiff of tear gas, the "pop-pop" of small-arms fire, these are smells and sounds that don't seem quite real – a sure sign that they are. Meanwhile, back on the valley road, soldiers lean against their jeeps waiting for their turn at the action.

We turn west after Shiloh, and just past the massive settlement of Ariel we reach the outskirts of Haris, surrounded by its olive groves. The village is tiny, insignificant. It has been under curfew for a week and no end in sight. The one entrance road is blocked with a huge pile of rock and earth, bulldozed by the IDF to close the way, so no one will think of breaking the curfew by driving in or out. All around us, a sea of olive trees groans with the weight of unpicked fruit. The harvesters can't work while the barricade stands.

There is a small bus with a dove-for-peace logo parked at the village entrance, and sure enough, a group of a dozen Israelis is there, shoulder to shoulder with a much larger contingent of Palestinian men and boys. They are trying hard to clear the road, attacking the earthen barricade with picks and shovels. "Something there is that does not love a wall."

A small force of Israeli soldiers are eyeing the action warily, heavily armed with M16's and tear-gas launchers. Then there is the media. Like my journalist friend, folks have been doing their homework. Israeli peaceniks working with Palestinians to harvest olives is just maybe a story; four or five reporters and a couple of TV cameras are taking in every detail. Things are just beginning to look ugly. The big crowd of Palestinian youths is glaring at the army with a kind of determination you might see on a football field. The Israeli activists are standing very close to the Palestinians, not allowing any sense of "them" and "us." The army guys don't like it, not one little bit.

Near the barricade, a slightly older Palestinian man is giving a brief little speech, both in Arabic and English. These Israeli peace folks, he reminds everyone, are the guests of our village, and they are to be protected. Not one of the Arab youths should even think of lifting a stone, he says. Everyone knows what will happen then, and if the soldiers start shooting, the Israeli guests are in the line of fire. This must not happen, he says, looking directly at the youngest boys present. And everyone listens, not a single hand strays down to the earth where the stones lie temptingly in the slanting light.

The army is there to keep the barricade in place, and the demonstrators are there to remove it. What is at stake here? On the one hand, army protection for Jewish settlers driving by, and, on the other, this village's entire olive harvest. The road is the key, and no one will give in. It is a standoff. Two blue-uniformed Israeli police officers start to expostulate with the Israeli peaceniks, who are looking remarkably like 1960s anti-nuke demonstrators from, say, Concord, New Hampshire. A few have long hair, streaked with gray, and there are some embroidered vests, and the ring-leaders are two younger Israeli women who are not keeping quiet. One of these is being interviewed by CNN about the disregard for human rights and the dangerous results of the Occupation that we are seeing before our very eyes. The other is arguing with the police officer about the fine points of army arrests for civil disobedience. An IDF military order designating the area a "Closed Military Zone" is being brandished about by the police, and she demands to see it. The officer claims that this order means that all the Israelis have to leave immediately. The feisty activist, waving a bunch of wildflowers in one hand and the creased order in the other, counters that the order is illegal because it lacks a signature, and therefore doesn't mean a damn thing. Everyone takes a look, all the TV cameras zoom in and get the order up close. Sure enough – no signature. Looks like they'll just have to arrest everyone without benefit of paperwork.

The argument goes on for a while, and then the police officer says, "Arrest them please;" I am struck by how polite it sounds. Five soldiers move in closer. Feisty Wildflowers is the first to be knocked down and dragged around a bit, resisting energetically, until they finally let her go. In a dramatic move that remains imprinted in my memory, she picks herself up and vaults gracefully over the earthen barricade, her long hair streaming as she runs to join the group of Palestinians waiting on the other side. She speaks quietly with them, and together they move through the groves toward the village beyond, vanishing from the camera lens, like a story not ready to be told.

Meanwhile the solders and police have knocked down another couple of Israeli protesters, both men, arresting them roughly and marching them off to the waiting jeep. The rest of the protesters are shoved back, at gunpoint, until they all board their bus. They are going back to Jerusalem. It is all over.

My journalist friend and I drive away, and around the bend we find a few Palestinians trying furtively to pick a few of the olives from their trees, just in sight of the nearby settlement. An old Arab woman is making her way across the road from the "forbidden" grove, where the Israelis and Palestinians have abandoned their joint effort for the day. The lone woman, stooped and gray, clutches a great heap of olives to her breast, hidden well under her embroidered dress. As we talk with her, we hear again the unbelievable tale of settlers destroying the groves, beating the villagers, uprooting the trees, rampaging with guns in the village by night. As she speaks, the woman's lined features are touched by the afternoon light, gold and heavy. Her face glows with tears and human beauty, and with the sheer relief she clearly feels to be talking with strangers who carry only cameras, not guns. She is as ancient as the trees, and she is headed home with a few olives gleaned from the family grove. As if to prove her tale, and to seal our afternoon with an incongruous hope, she reaches, without the slightest embarrassment, deep within the bosom of her dress, drawing forth to offer to us with both hands heaps of smooth and oily fruit, and they glow too.

SOME HOLY BULLIES
Jerusalem, 21st February 2002

If you are one of the lucky folk whose house is not surrounded by tanks, it's a good idea to get out of the un-Holy Land every once in a while. Last month, after a refreshing time away in England, I found myself flying back to Tel Aviv on KLM when my seatmate struck up a conversation. She was an American Jewish woman, young, observant, and had noticed that I was reading Karen Armstrong's book on religious fundamentalism.

"Are you interested in religion?" she asked.

"Well, actually, yes..." I told her about the courses I teach in Jerusalem on biblical studies, the history of Israel and Palestine and contemporary issues. I tried to keep it neutral. But she was way ahead of me.

"We wouldn't be having so much trouble with the Arabs if we would pray more and follow the Bible."

I completely agreed. I told her about my admiration for the prophet Amos with his call for justice and compassion, especially for the poor and the stranger.

I had really struck out. My seatmate was bristling.

"In fact," she informed me, "God told us to kill all the Canaanites when we came into the Land of Israel, and we didn't do what we were told. Now look at the trouble we are in."

She actually turned up her nose at me, as she went back to her prayer book.

"Oh," I said.

At the Amsterdam airport I had a little time between flights, so I went to look at the souvenirs. Wooden shoes, windmill trinkets, boxes of chocolate. I ran into an Israeli family, or would have if I had not flattened myself against the wall as they barged past me, oblivious of my existence. Their conversation was enlightening:

Dad (stocky, muscular, tanned, maybe ex-commando with slight paunch): "We'd better get back to the gate, the security questions for the Tel Aviv flight will take some time."

Mom (hair henna-ed, big bracelets): "I'm glad we got the cute chocolate windmills for auntie. Say, what should I do with this Dutch money I have left over?"

Daughter (anorexic version of Mom, naked midriff, stud through nose): "Hey, Mom, here's a charity collection box of some kind with coins in it…"

Dad: "What's it say on it? 'Amnesty International: Working for Human Rights.' Humph. No way! We're not giving those jerks any of our money, they're badmouthing us at the UN and all over the place."

Son (Leninesque goatee and wire-rims): "Those idiots. I'll give them a piece of my fist, that's what!" Which he does, slamming the plastic Amnesty International collection box until it practically falls over.

On they go to the gate. On to Tel Aviv. On home to the Middle East's only enlightened democracy.

•

Back in East Jerusalem, I sleep fitfully. The IDF Border Patrol jeeps are revving their motors up and down Saladdin Street outside my window. Someone shouts something in Arabic, and there is a mysterious flurry of running footsteps. Silence. I dream I am in a demonstration against the Occupation. We are all in Jerusalem but it feels like London. Two lines have formed, facing off. Soldiers hold British flags. Suddenly I understand that it is a contra dance forming up; everyone is holding hands, dancing down the street.

The ringing of the phone jolts me awake. My colleague at work, Daoud, has been detained by the army at a checkpoint while crossing from the West Bank into Jerusalem. The IDF has handed him over to the police, and they are booking him at the Police Station *cum* Border Patrol Headquarters on the top floor of the old East Jerusalem Post Office. Daoud's voice is quiet but urgent. Can I come over there right away? Down the street I go.

Up the dank stairs at the station, I find Daoud with another dozen Arab men who had been apprehended on their way to a construction job in Israel. They wear plastic wrist-cuffs. Police officers are going in and out, ignoring requests for information. It turns out we are waiting for the ID cards of all the men to arrive; they apparently got "lost" in the Army jeep *en route*. When the ID's arrive, each of the men will be interrogated separately.

A tough-looking policewoman asks me: "Who are you?"

"I'm representing Daoud's employer."

"Okay, wait over there. We will want to interrogate you too."

Great. We all wait. Two hours pass. No progress. I go back and forth from desk to desk. Nothing. We just wait.

In mid-morning a bunch of soldiers roar up, park their jeep in the street below and run up the stairs with a Palestinian man in tow. They push him through the hall where we are standing, and on the way one of the soldiers, a short guy with a long M-16, kicks him repeatedly behind the knees. The Palestinian man stumbles, but keeps his balance and is pushed toward the interrogation room. I find myself inexplicably standing in the way, blocking their path. Without intending to, I'm shouting:

"Hey, what's going on here? What're you doing? You can't just kick people around like that. I'm here, I see you! I see what you're doing. Stop kicking him!"

I'm beside myself with rage, not sure what I'm saying. The soldiers stare coldly. As they push by me, I follow them toward the interrogation room, still shouting at them. A female soldier standing in the hall glares at me, but says nothing, just rolling her eyes to the ceiling and turning away. Suddenly I realize that Daoud is gripping my arm tightly and talking to me, telling me to calm down, pulling me back to the hallway, making me sit down. I'm shaking. I'm holding back the tears, embarrassed. Eventually, somehow, we get out of there, and Daoud walks me home. I'm glad he's there.

●

Someone has just written a book entitled *Muscular Christianity* – a sociological study of the intense appeal that a fusion of strength and religion exercised in the mainstream American Protestant tradition in the early 20th century. People like Teddy Roosevelt were role models from the "bully pulpit" of the White House for Americans who forthwith sent their kids off to schools that were virtual Christian boot camps.

It only takes a little imagination, and a look at Germany in the 1930s, to see where "muscular Christianity" could have led more of American society, if it were not for the balancing forces of ethnic and religious diversity that transformed America in the post-war years. Would it be at all surprising to see "muscular Christianity" making a comeback after 9/11?

"Muscular Judaism" is having a field day in Israel. We are all likely to think that this is a healthy change from the Diaspora stereotype of the helpless ghetto dweller kicked around by the anti-Semitic Gentile world. I have had opportunity to celebrate the emergence of the "new Jew" who is nobody's scapegoat. I will never forget my first encounter with Israeli kids on the kibbutz, thirty years ago. We were swimming in the kibbutz pool, and a dozen of those little "new Jews" dived on top of me and pushed me under until I yelled, "I surrender!" It was my first sentence in colloquial Hebrew. I learned it fast and still remember it. As a result, I didn't get drowned.

Those kibbutz kids have all grown up to become good strong healthy boys and girls, with M16's and Apache helicopters, doing their duty and defending their divinely given homeland from the remnants of the barbaric Canaanites. We know that we should applaud the creation of an assertive and self-reliant Jewish identity – but where in God's name is it going?

When I was in fifth grade I avoided the class bully. I was tall for my age but never had any muscle to speak of. I saw myself as a scrawny farm boy, and acted that way. One day I came home in tears because the bully had been doing his thing, and my father took me out to the barn, hung a grain sack from a beam, and showed me how to punch. It felt great. I faced down the bully and was never bothered by him again. That felt good too. No one likes to be kicked behind the knees.

Where is the balance between wisdom and force? All night we hear the thud of massive explosions as the Israeli Air Force, using muscular American technology, destroys the infrastructure of the Palestinian Authority. IDF checkpoints strangle the villages. A thousand times a day, Israelis with guns humiliate unarmed men, women and children, pushing their faces into the mud of a stolen land. Tanks in Ramallah flex their steel biceps. Blue and white flags wave confidently over Israeli settlements in conquered Canaan.

These are illusions of strength. We know what is required, and this is not it. If religion teaches that Jews own everything in sight and have a divine mandate to dispossess the Arabs, then that kind of religion will bring disaster on Israel. If Israeli citizens are told that Zionism means wallowing in self-pity for being hated by the world while denying human rights to 3 million Palestinians, then Zionist isolationists will simply put on more and more mindless muscle. There is no wisdom in this, and no real religion either. There is certainly no safety in this holy bullying. As Israel's leaders call for national unity and determination, Israeli soldiers and armed settlers are daily attacked by Palestinian gunmen, while Israeli citizens are killed by men and (now) women wrapped in explosives. Is anyone really surprised that scrawny kids can learn to kick back?

Holy bullies are not essentially any more sophisticated than the playground variety. If we weren't so terrified, any one of us could call their bluff. You do not have to be a strategic analyst to realize that those who feel threatened by terrorism do not have a monopoly on the right to self-defense. You do not have to be a political scientist to understand that a prolonged military occupation of an entire people will not make them your friends, or your servants. You do not have to be a theologian to know that a self-righteous "crusade" against a local "axis of evil" is a dangerous fantasy, not religious patriotism. And you do not have to be a biblical scholar to understand exactly what the prophet Amos is talking about:

> Woe to those who are at ease in Zion, and to those who feel secure on the mountain of Samaria... Because you trample the poor... you will build houses of hewn stone and not live in them... Seek good, and not evil, that you may live...and establish justice in the gates.

HALFWAY WORDS
Jerusalem, 9th March 2002

On Saturday March 2nd, in the evening, our windows rattled and walls shook as the Palestinian suicide bomber blew himself up across the highway in the Orthodox neighborhood of Beit Yisrael. It was the end of the Sabbath; hundreds of observant residents were exiting synagogues and *yeshivot*. Women, children and men of all ages died instantly or were rushed to the hospital in pieces. Blood was on the sidewalk and splashed up the walls of buildings.

Soon we all knew that the bomber was from the Deheisheh refugee camp, south of Bethlehem. I called a Palestinian colleague in Deheisheh whom I have known for years. His wife answered the phone and I could hear their kids in the background. I could picture the tiny living room, the little kitchenette, clean and neat and sparse. As I pressed the receiver to my ear, I could feel my hand shaking, and my voice sounded strange to myself as I asked him to talk to me about the bomber and the bombing.

"We condemn any such killing of civilians," he said immediately. "I personally am opposed to any Palestinian attacks inside Israel, but I have to tell you honestly that I support attacks on Israeli soldiers and settlers in the Occupied Territories. This is a *sort of* war. No one can say what is right and what is wrong. These actions are the only way Palestinians see that they can fight the Occupation. And things will only get worse. This stupid man Israel has chosen to lead them, does anyone know what he is after? He is making a big mistake, pushing us, pushing us until we all explode, with nothing left to lose..."

Monday was a black day. Prime Minister Sharon addressed a plenum of the *Kenesset*, telling the nation that "the Palestinians have to be hit hard. If they aren't badly beaten there won't be any negotiations. I want an agreement, but first they have to be beaten. It's us or them." During the day, Israeli forces, operating under orders from Sharon in what he called a "continuous campaign" in his "long and difficult war" against Palestine, killed sixteen Palestinians and wounded thirty. In the Jenin refugee camp, six Palestinians were killed. Two of these were armed and returning fire; the rest, apparently, were unarmed, including the Palestinian woman who was struck by helicopter fire inside her home, and the Red Cross doctor who was killed trying to reach her. Just after 1 p.m., tank shells fired from Israeli positions hit a pick-up truck in El Bireh, instantly killing a 38-year-old Arab woman and her three children as she drove them home from school. An Israeli Army spokesman apologized, saying the tank gunners had made a mistake.

Anyone who might have been trying to make sense of events on the blood-dimmed stage of Israel and Palestine has by this time given up. Still, although totally incomprehensible, the scenario is crazily predictable. It does not take much imagination to reconstruct each horrible day – "unbridled brutality" really does not quite say it. Madness rules around the clock, and revenge never sleeps. On Monday night, just after 2 a.m., a former Palestinian navy officer took up a position on a pedestrian bridge in Tel Aviv and fired an M16 into a crowded restaurant, killing three civilians instantly and wounding thirty-six, before an Israeli Druze police officer wrestled him to the ground even as the man knifed him to death.

How can words possibly report these things? The brute facts have finally choked me. I hear words that tell only anger and anguish, never the whole truth. I feel my hands moving to block the voices, to protect my ears. The silence looms, and I fear it.

> The bearer of evil tidings,
> When he was halfway there,
> Remembered that evil tidings
> Are a dangerous thing to bear.

In Robert Frost's poem, the messenger remembers in time, and saves himself. I have not been able to do that, and so I have missed the peaceful benefits that this clever fellow found in the

Tibetan paradise to which he turned aside. One of the lesser dangers of being a messenger of bad news is that people will be angry with you. Writing an essay about bad behavior among Israelis, I am called an anti-Semite and a racist. Standing with the Women in Black at the junction of two streets in Jerusalem, holding a sign saying *"End the Occupation,"* I hear the passing drivers yelling: "Murderer! Traitor! Whore!"

Disconcerting. But hatred by others is not the main danger. No, the real risk of carrying evil tidings is the corrosive effect of the message on the messenger. Day after day, watching people I love overcome by despair and the desire for revenge, my heart has not remained steady. I too have been overcome; there is no pretending otherwise. As I go back and read the well-intentioned words I have written over the last sixteen months, I see the innocence of grieving giving way to the edge of irony, irony becoming bitterness, and bitterness bordering on... What? Despair? Apathy? Bigotry?

I stand between Israel and Palestine, unable to keep my heart clear and open. I have not told the whole truth. I never completed that essay I intended to write about my visit to the Hadera hospital, where elderly Jewish women lay scarred by a terrorist bus bomb. They looked silently at me from their beds. I gradually left them behind. There were a thousand details I never wrote, each of them precious and unique, like the Israeli soldier at the Bethlehem checkpoint who asked me to pray for him... I let his story fade. I turned away from the tale of teenage Israeli boys bludgeoned in a desert cave, of the 72-year-old Jewish man murdered in Bethlehem. I passed by the story of the 15-year-old girl wounded by a terrorist bomb in Tel Aviv, who woke after a week in coma, convinced that she was in the hospital to give birth to a baby girl...

Too many stories. Too much pain. I made my choices, and my unspoken message condemns me. I sifted my reactions, manipulated my perception, slanted my vision. I looked for the villains and the heroes, and I found them. Why? My emotions conquered me, the message bruised me, the burden of the whole truth was too heavy for me.

I had hopes, and my hopes were disappointed. On March 1st, the Palestinian weekly *Jerusalem Times* published an opinion piece by Elias Tuma on nonviolent resistance:

> To abandon violence does not mean abandoning the goals of independence and statehood... The struggle to realize these objectives may be intensified, but without violence: no firearms, no stabbing, no stone throwing, and certainly...no suicide bombing, whether against soldiers or civilians.

There was a time when words like these would warm my heart, now they just make me sad. I tell myself that this is a good message, but my heart just can't believe.

I had a visit from a French activist who spent some time in the Aida refugee camp in Bethlehem, working on an original initiative with some members of the Palestinian factions PFLP and Hamas. The idea was to translate a book of Dr. Martin Luther King's sayings into colloquial Arabic. Things were going fine, my visitor reported, until they reached some passages about nonviolence and loving one's enemy. At that point, the Palestinian translators started getting uncomfortable. Delays started to crop up. One day the chief translator got a stern lecture from his uncle, warning him not to have anything to do with any work that might favor "normalization" with the Israelis. The poor translator immediately got so ill he could not continue. That was the end of the Arabic *Quotes of Dr. King*.

Now, of course, the Israeli Army has occupied the Aida refugee camp with tanks, and everyone is busy shooting and being shot. The thoughts of MLK on nonviolence will not be reaching these particular Palestinians. Anyway, what relevance could the thoughts of a black southern preacher have to their real lives?

Everything conspires to keep his message from them – including their desire not to hear it.

"The truth will set you free." We might have chosen truth, but we invented instead a halfway language. Israelis call into public radio stations and say that Arabs are animals and should be exterminated, while Israeli officials report attacks on "terrorist targets" (where large numbers of civilians are killed), and apologize for their more obvious mistakes. A Palestinian student informs me that "all Jews are the same," and a Palestinian university professor tells me that Muslims can consider suicide bombers as freedom fighters, since they are attacking the enemy (even when the "enemy" are unarmed teenagers studying at their desks). I hear all these things, and I feel angry and betrayed, but can no longer blame the speakers. All our hearts have been corroded and hardened by the evil tidings we bear.

Halfway words are all we have. Still, half-heartedly, we know the truth: conquest will not set us free. As our power to be compassionate falters, the Occupation and its consequences continue killing us all. Jews and Arabs, Israelis and Palestinians, have swallowed enough evil tidings to destroy the souls of both nations, and still neither has the courage to loosen the deadly grip. Silenced by dishonesty, we send more kids with guns to spread the rule of state terror and the rule of partisan terror – all for nothing but to defend the Occupation, or destroy it. Then, silenced by grief, we bury the dead. If another more honest witness does not step in, the lines of battle will soon pass through every classroom and bedroom in this land. Someone must redraw the border between sanity and cruelty; already we have forgotten where that boundary once stood.

Meanwhile, Israeli children try to hide their fear behind their parents' flags, while the children of Palestine shiver mutely in their beds when the night grows dark, and the shooting resumes along an invisible frontier.

LETTER TO A MUSLIM COLLEAGUE
Jerusalem, 29th March 2002 – Good Friday

Dear M.,

On Wednesday evening, as over 200 guests sat down to the Jewish Passover *Seder* Meal at the Park Hotel in Netanya, a Palestinian man with explosives wrapped around him stepped into the dining room and blew himself up. He killed over twenty, wounded over one hundred. His victims included women, children, and elderly, as well as able-bodied men whom he might have regarded as enemy soldiers. Today, just a few minutes ago, as I was writing this, another Palestinian – this time a woman – blew herself up in a Jerusalem supermarket, killing and wounding a number (as yet unclear) of Israeli shoppers. Such attacks are becoming our daily fare.

I know that you condemn these acts. Or do I? You and I have been involved in interfaith work for years; we have taught and traveled together. We have shared moments of prayer and hope together. But do we really know each other? I am a Christian theologian, you are a Muslim theologian. I have shared with you my admiration for the mysticism of Gregory of Nyssa, you have told me of the lyrical mysticism of the Sufi poetess Rabi'a. We both live in Jerusalem, we both have young children to worry about and to hope for. As teachers, we both care about the health of the spirit and the mind, as well as the safety of the body. But when it comes to acts of terror, are we living on separate planets of belief?

Not so long ago, while teaching, you responded to a question about suicide terrorism. I think I heard you say that many Muslims do not see "suicide bombings" as "suicide" at all. You said, I think, that many Muslims regard these "actions" as the equivalent of a warrior throwing himself against the enemy lines, knowing he will not survive, but determined to kill some of the enemy as well. Mustafa, I need to ask you – is this how you yourself see acts of suicide terror? I need your answer, because I need to know the truth. Help me to understand.

Today, Sharon's Army of Occupation surrounds Arafat's headquarters in Ramallah, and during these very minutes as I am writing to you, fierce exchanges of gunfire are killing armed men on both sides, and I have no doubt that casualties include unarmed people as well – this is the way this ugly conflict is going. I know that you will condemn the decision by Israel's leaders to isolate, discredit, physically assault and essentially declare war on the entire Palestinian people. I know that you also condemn the acts of violence against Palestinian civilians, men, women and children, in the Occupied Territories during the past months of upheaval. I know that you mourn with me, and with anyone who works for peace, as we all see our hopes of peace destroyed by stubborn and vindictive leaders, and by the terror and hatred they have nurtured in their people.

It is my belief that in all this we share a common spiritual conviction. We are both theologians, not politicians. We can both see, or at least try to see, our human actions and words in the light of something more beautiful and gracious and true than the mess we are in. It does not matter if we call that "something" God or Christ, Allah or the Holy Spirit. Whatever our vocabulary, we can both believe that we have been given our religious traditions, your Islam and my Christianity, not to inspire hatred and suspicion, but to inspire us to compassion and courage. But, I wonder, when outrages are committed against our common and divinely given humanity, do you and I really respond in the same spiritual language? If so, do we not need to unite our voices better?

Every day, in the Israeli press, I find Jewish Israeli writers who utterly condemn the Israeli Occupation of Palestinian land and the destruction of Palestinian lives. I count some Jewish Israeli peace activists among my most trusted colleagues. These are people of wisdom, who know that every "enemy" is first and foremost a human being, created in the divine image. Where are the similar voices from the "other side"?

I need your help in understanding why I have not heard a single Muslim condemn in unequivocal terms the murder of those people in Netanya or those shoppers in Jerusalem. People unarmed and undefended. People, like you and me, trying for a moment to put aside their fear. People just sitting down with their families to eat a meal. People who just that moment had begun to pray. That, as you well know, is what the Passover *Seder* is for the Jewish people: a way to pray. That prayer has been cut off. Torn prayer books lie open on the shattered tables. The Exodus story, the sharing of unleavened bread and bitter herbs – all these are prayer, and it has been cut off. Who can restore a murdered prayer? If we ever pray ourselves, we must ask this.

Some years ago, an Israeli Jewish fundamentalist, Dr. Baruch Goldstein, entered the mosque of Abraham in Hebron, shooting at the gathered worshippers, killing and maiming at will, until he was overcome. I know that to this day some Israelis refuse, incredibly, to condemn that act of barbarity. They regard that man as a "martyr" and a "hero" for killing Arabs at prayer. You know how revolted I am that anyone could applaud such an act of hatred, in the name of religion, in the name of God.

If this were Ireland, and if we were talking about Catholics and Protestants, my own theological responses to all this would be more relevant. But here in Jerusalem, the religious issues are very different; Judaism and Islam are the majority narratives of faith. So, when Abdel-Baset Odeh, who killed on Passover Eve in Netanya, is praised as a "martyr," the opinion of a Christian theologian is not relevant. I need to hear a Muslim voice.

I know the complexity of Palestinian attitudes toward resistance. Violent struggle is an issue that I, as a non-Palestinian, cannot resolve. But, as a Christian theologian who lives in Jerusalem, whose children run the same risks from terror that all children run, I know that I am right to ask some questions. I turn to you – precisely because of your theological perspective. As a Muslim theologian, as a man of faith and an advocate of peace, you are the only one I can turn to. It is responses of faith and humanity, not the cynical answers of politics and strategy, which I need. Sharon can condemn terrorism, and continue to terrorize on a state-sponsored level. Arafat can say that suicide attacks against Israelis are "inadvisable" and still praise the "martyrdom" of young suicide bombers. Sharon and Arafat cannot speak to my soul. They are old warriors, and their words are about the victory of force, not truth.

That is why I am asking you to speak to me. I believe that the political aspects of this ugly struggle will be resolved, and that two nations will dwell side by side, in a bitterly earned peace. What I cannot believe today is that our minds and hearts can survive the intensity of hatred that too many Jews and Muslims will bring with them into that future. If it does not kill us, this hatred will destroy our souls. It is for the souls that I am asking you to speak, even as the bodies are destroyed.

I desperately need to hear your voice. We are theologians, not politicians; can we not offer gifts of sanctity to each other? Tell me how a Muslim speaks out against violence that kills people at prayer, against premeditated slaughter that kills people while they shop for food. Tell me, with a faithful Muslim voice, how Islam prepares the human heart to look beyond revenge, to look beyond the cycle of retaliation, to understand the suffering of all of Abraham's children equally. Tell me how the compassion of Islam offers a path of truth to transcend that suffering with acts of wisdom. Bring me a message of comfort from your faith, and show me a way that leads beyond acts of stark despair, beyond courage that is only brutal, not holy.

Salamat wa'Salawat,
Henry R. Carse

BANALITIES AND BLESSINGS
Jerusalem, 9th May 2002

From Western Easter to Eastern Easter, for five long weeks in the warming springtime of the Promised Land, as the anemones and poppies have been blooming, sordid and brutal events have been unfolding all around us. Anyone can see that news and views are all over the map; no one can guess what cruel absurdities and griefs lie ahead. Still, can we dare to count our blessings?

On Easter Sunday, the last day of March, I visited friends in Beit Sahour on the outskirts of Bethlehem. I arrived at the Orthodox Church and found the place overflowing with worshippers. For Orthodox Christians this was just another Sunday during Lent, but the church was so packed that I could barely squeeze into the gate. Kids were all over the place, dressed to the nines. A bunch of official-looking fellows showed up outside the church hanging big Palestinian flags and photos of Arafat on the church fence, then adding a long banner featuring the Palestinian President. Children played peek-a-boo behind the banners and the flags, and one kid rushed around handing out photos of dead Palestinian heroes, all inscribed with the word *SHAHEED* – martyr.

As the last blessings were intoned from the church, crowds were already gathering in the street for the Big Rally. This was in support of Arafat, confined as he was to his offices in Ramallah, surrounded by Israeli tanks. It was also a general demonstration of resistance to Israeli incursions into Palestinian areas. There was no doubt that people here were expecting an imminent Israeli invasion into the streets of Bethlehem, Beit Sahour and Beit Jala, towns already familiar with occupation, resistance, firefights, assassinations, retaliations, and dread.

My host, Suzan, is employed by the Palestinian municipality of Beit Sahour. She and her 7-year-old daughter Luna joined me at the church door, and we walked through the thronged streets toward the equivalent of a town square. A few internationals and ex-pats were gathered here with the townsfolk. Under a banner praising the imprisoned "*Rais*," some town notables were giving short speeches. The bearded and handsome parish priest, in the impressive black robe of the Orthodox clergy, shouted out his address from under an array of local icons: Arafat in his *keffiyeh*, the Virgin Mary in a blue dress, and Saddam Hussein in a pressed uniform, gazing down benignly on the crowd.

Suzan treated me to a running commentary on local politics, while keeping an eye on her daughter scampering around through the crowd. Everyone was talking at once, speech or no speech. Just when I thought it could not get more chaotic, a youth who looked thirteen, with his head completely wrapped in a checked *keffiyeh*, climbed to the top of the nearest building and let off into the air an ear-splitting live round from his Kalashnikov. Jolted by the shooting, my hostess immediately rushed off to make sure Luna was okay. Some of the kids around me were cowering, tearful, against their parents, and not a few adults were shaking their heads and saying, "Why? Why?"

Why indeed? Shows of juvenile aggression translate well into patriotism in most Middle Eastern languages. But no amount of nationalist lingo can make firing guns over the heads of toddlers anything but banal.

Luna's mother returned through the crowd not only with Luna but with a *Tanzim* militia fighter she wanted me to meet. Atta, let's call him, was young, handsome, somewhat tense, obviously admired, and gracious. Suzan thought I might like to talk with Atta about human rights, since he had announced the formation of a Human Rights Committee for the local *Tanzim* under his command. Realizing that I had left all my notes on the *Tanzim* militias at home, I *ad libbed* with a few questions about the concept of "purity of arms." After some tricky translation footwork, the question finally reached him: As a commander of armed

Palestinian men, what were his directives concerning the use of weapons or explosives against Israeli civilians?

"Absolutely forbidden!" Atta was adamant. "I train my men to fight the Israeli Army. They are forbidden to attack civilians, anywhere. Not even in the illegal Israeli settlements."

Atta and his men had their chance to practice what they preached. On April 2nd, 2002, the IDF invaded Bethlehem. Five weeks later, when I returned to Beit Sahour, Suzan and her family were under house arrest. Little Luna had put her head out the window one morning to find tanks in the street and an Israeli soldier with his gun pointed at her face, she crawled under her bed and didn't speak a word for two days. Neighbors were harassed and their houses trashed, others disappeared into military prisons, and over a hundred of Atta's colleagues were besieged by Israeli forces inside the Church of the Nativity

Orthodox Easter came. I had promised to visit my friends to mark the feast, so I made my way over incongruous roads to their home, where I found the entire family gathered. I brought them festive chocolates, cheese and some of my *"intifada* chip cookies" and we ate and talked. One of Luna's uncles engaged me in a conversation about the Israeli occupation and Palestinian resistance. After a while, I asked him about the word *shaheed* – martyr. What does this mean to Palestinians?

"Oh," he said, "anyone who dies fighting the enemy is a martyr."

"What about people who blow themselves up, killing Israeli civilians. Are they fighting the enemy?"

He leaned closer and told me a little secret: "There are no Israeli civilians. Everyone knows that they all serve in the army, from the age of eighteen to the age of fifty-six."

"Oh," I said. "What about babies, and old people?"

"Look," he said, angry now, "do you think any of us condone these things?"

Language can stretch just so far, and then it snaps.

I am slowly learning the true meaning of banality. I once thought that the word simply means uninteresting. But "banal" comes from an old French word denoting "compulsory feudal service." Exactly. Israelis and Palestinians are trapped in the compulsory service of a benighted master. "Nationalism is an infantile disease," wrote Albert Einstein. If so, this house we share uneasily – and call "Israel/Palestine" – is a vast curfewed hospital for miserably ill infant nationalists.

Nationalism does things to communication. A correspondent for *Haaretz* did a revealing study of Israel Radio's guidelines on vocabulary in its Arabic broadcasts. Statements by Israeli government spokespersons, for example, cannot be called "versions" because this seems to cast some doubt on their veracity. A member of the Israeli Parliament cannot "refute" or "contradict" the Prime Minister. No, the right phrase is "expressed his objections." And, most importantly, "victim" must never be used to refer to a Palestinian civilian – he or she is simply "dead."

My love for words is such that I hate to see them brutalized. Even wordless images are here pressed into the service of mindless politics. A bizarre (and very banal) example comes from the dusty margins of the Jenin fiasco. About the recent Israeli incursion into the Palestinian city of Jenin, what we know for sure is very little. Our ignorance will not bring back the dead, or turn back the clock, but maybe it will give us pause. In the words of an Israeli journalist: "Okay, so there wasn't a massacre. Israel only shot some children, brought a house crashing down on an old man, rained cement blocks on an invalid...used locals as human shields against bombs, and prevented aid from getting to the sick and wounded. That's really not a massacre."

One day, as the experts argued semantics, an Israeli Army spokesperson announced evidence of Palestinians in Jenin staging "fake burials." An Israeli intelligence plane filmed some Palestinians carrying a stretcher, and another Palestinian with a camera filming the stretcher-bearers as they made their way toward the cemetery. The man on the stretcher, however, fell off twice, and nimbly climbed back on as the little procession proceeded. The conclusion reached by the Israeli Army: the Palestinians were staging funerals as "evidence" of killings by Israeli forces, killings that did not occur in "real life."

The banality of this episode can only be truly appreciated when one reads the Palestinian response. Oh, yes, there were people filming in that place, just as the record shows. Yes indeed! This was, in fact, a Palestinian film crew making a movie about a Palestinian funeral: a little slice of local cinema with a relevant theme. In other words, this was not Palestinians faking a funeral for the purposes of anti-Israel propaganda... No, this was *art!*

Can anyone tell me what blessings might emerge to be counted out of such a sea of dissemblance? Since the first bloody days of this *Intifada*, I have been putting my words to paper, hoping that they will be blessings of a sort. I have found only glimpses of goodness, but they have been enough to keep my heart from despair, as the sirens sound in Netanya and the bus bombs echo in Jerusalem, as the dust settles over Jenin and the sordid truth emerges from the shadows of Bethlehem, like the poet's "rough beast, its time come round at last." Even a single blessing deserves counting.

Unexpectedly, a miracle came my way. Imagine a small group of Palestinian and Israeli parents meeting in Jerusalem for the first time, sitting around a table, sharing coffee, discussing a shared future for their kids. Actually, what if their shared future were to begin *today*? What if twelve Jewish and Arab children between the ages of 10 and 12 could be lifted out of the conflict zone for a week or so, fly to a neutral place, get to know each other as far more than "enemies," and enjoy each others' company at a summer camp with a focus on peace?

What if? The question became a dream, the dream a plan, and before we knew it, here were twelve pairs of cautious but hopeful Jerusalem parents – Jews, Christians and Muslims, from both sides of the wall of fear – willing to talk it over, and courageous enough to entrust their kids to an experiment in "education for peace."

I watched, speechless, as if a celestial apparition had suddenly shone into my neighborhood. These Israelis and Palestinians, who simply do not accept the imposed "state of war" between them, who care about the hearts and souls of their kids, and about a sane future for all, cannot be stopped or silenced by the banality of hate.

This little project may be new, but the idea is as old as time. Children, and only children, can write a new script when the violence reaches its peak. Even the biblical Isaac and Ishmael, brothers and life-long rivals, were reconciled when the day came to bury Abraham their father. Bring the kids together, let them learn to trust each other, even as the adults have failed. Will the children of the Holy Land have the means to bury our grievous errors in the rich forgiving soil of their respect for each other, and for life?

I can't yet know if this will be just another hope disappointed, whether these children of Abraham gathering here, ready to be friends, will be the true survivors of a time of darkness in Israel and Palestine. I will allow myself this thought: maybe all that we have suffered here together was just the breaking of the rocky earth for these very seeds.

In another time, there was another Abraham, a simple and profound man, who had to see, as we now see, the price paid by brothers for injustices endured through generations of mutual bondage. In 1862, Abraham Lincoln wrote that "in the present civil war it is quite possible that God's purpose is something different from the purpose of either party." Although he led one side, Lincoln could transcend his own agenda and think beyond nationalism. Three years later, as the slaughter neared its end, Lincoln wrote words that could perhaps be spoken today from the devastated rubble in Jenin or the smoldering ruins in Rishon LeTsion:

> Both parties deprecated war; but one of them
> would make war rather than let the nation survive;
> the other would accept war rather than let it perish.

We are not yet ready for the wisdom of his words, although our children might be. Abraham Lincoln had the audacity to see a hidden blessing in a banal conflict. It was not the victory of one side or the other that gave him hope, but the reconciliation he desired. He had a vision that is lacking today on the ideological battlegrounds of Jerusalem, Ramallah, Bethlehem and Tel Aviv, but which, if we act wisely, may yet be encouraged in our children. Education for peace, a summer camp, some shared quality time for our war-shocked kids...this may be all we can manage while the tanks and bombs seem to drown out reason.

But when the shooting stops, as it will one day, what then? If these same children have been nourished with the blessings of each other, not the banality of hatred and suspicion, then young Israelis and Palestinians may yet find the heart and the strength to build an entirely different kind of future, "with malice toward none, with charity for all...to do all which may achieve and cherish a just and a lasting peace."

REFERENCES

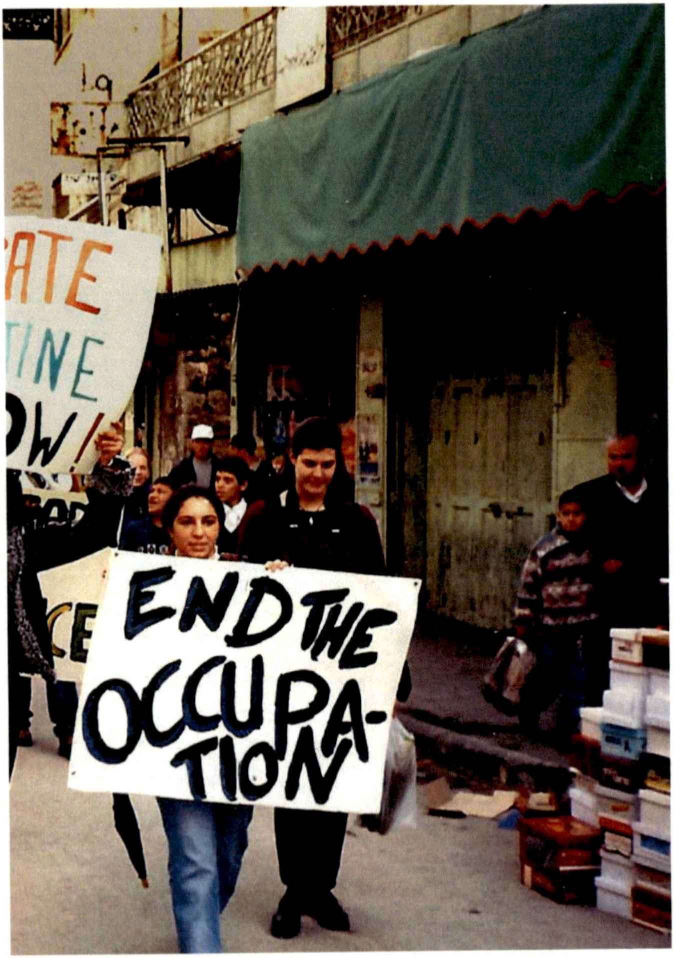
END THE OCCUPA-TION

REFERENCES

DREAMS OR NIGHTMARES
Yehuda Amichai, *Poems of Jerusalem*, 1988

NOVEMBER IN JERUSALEM
Rabbis for Human Rights (www.rhr.org)
Coalition of Women for Peace (www.coalitionofwomen.org)
Sabeel Ecumenical Liberation Theology Center (www.sabeel.org)
Mubarak Awad, "Nonviolence in the Occupied Territories," undated [1988]
"*Landolatry*" thanks to Yehezkel Landau

SOME BAD WIZARDS
Frank L. Baum, editorial in *Aberdeen Saturday Pioneer*, January 3, 1891

CAGES
Christian Peacemaker Teams (www.cpt.org)

A WALK IN NO-ONE LAND
B'tselem, Jerusalem: Injustice in the Holy City, 1999
Yehuda Amichai, "Tourists," in *Selected Poems*, 2000

GET THE CONNECTION
Arnold Mindell, *Sitting in the Fire*, 1995

FROM A DISTANCE
Haaretz, November 20, 2000
Robert Frost, "Mending Wall," in *Collected Poems, Prose and Plays*, 1995

LETTER TO A PALESTINIAN CHRISTIAN
Taylor Branch, *Pillar of Fire*, 1998

A HOME IN ANATA
Israeli Committee Against House Demolitions (www.icahd.org)
Jeremiah 30:18; 31:28
B'tselem Quarterly for Human Rights in the Occupied Territories,
1998

SOME PEOPLE MARCHING
Palestinian Center for Rapprochement (www.pcr.ps)
Applied Research Institute Jerusalem (www.arij.org)

PERFECTLY SAFE RUBBLE
Luke, Chapter 13

BOTH SIDES NOW
Thich Nhat Hanh, *Being Peace*, 2005

WHAT ABOUT THE KIDS?
B'Tselem – The Israeli Information Center for Human Rights
(www.btselem.org)
Iman Masarweh & Jamil Slahout, *The Suffering of Children Under Occupation*, 2002

AS IF
Fouad Ajami, "Commentary," *U.S. News & World Report*,
September 3, 2001

SOME HOLY BULLIES
Clifford Putney, *Muscular Christianity*, 2001
Amos, Chapter 6

HALFWAY WORDS
Robert Frost, "The Bearer of Evil Tidings" in *Collected Poems, Prose and Plays*, 1995
One Family Fund (www.onefamilyfund.org)
Israel Ministry of Foreign Affairs
(www.mfa.gov/MFA/Terrorism)

BANALITIES AND BLESSINGS
"Education for Peace" with Israeli and Palestinian Children: Kids4Peace (www.kids4peaceusa.org)
Abraham Lincoln, *Second Inaugural Address,* March 4, 1865